Cosmic Mysteries
A Fable

Jenny Koralek

Copyright © 2015 Jenny Koralek

All rights reserved.

Published by Toward Publishing

ISBN-13: 978-0-9931870-3-2

ABOUT THE AUTHOR

Jenny Koralek is an established children's author and editor, having had numerous books and short stories published over the past 35 years with, among others, Penguin, Hamish Hamilton, Walker Books, Frances Lincoln, CUP and Egmont in the UK and with various noted publishers in the USA.

In addition, several books have been translated into Danish, Dutch, Finnish, Greek, Italian and Norwegian.

She is also the author of *Mother, Do Not Weep for Me*, a memoir of her son's life and untimely death and co-editor of *A Lively Oracle, A Celebration of P L Travers, Creator of Mary Poppins*.

Initially inspired by her close friendship with P L Travers she became, alongside her writing career, a lifelong student of mythology and spiritual traditions

CONTENTS

Part One – Elizabeth	1
Part One – II	3
Part One - III	5
Part One - IV	15
Part Two - Maryam	19
Part Two - II	25
Part Two - III	31
Part Two - IV	37
Part Two - V	45
Part Two - VI	57
Part Two – VII	63
Part Two – VIII	71
Part Three – Elizabeth	89
Part Three – II	93
Part Three – III	101
Part Three – IV	109
Part Three – V	113
Part Three – VI	119
Part Three – VII	123
Part Three – VIII	129

Jenny Koralek

Part Three – IX	133
Part Three – X	139
Part Three – XI	147
Part Three – XII	155
Part Three – XIII	159
Part Three – XIV	163
Part Three – XV	167
Part Three – XVI	171
Part Three – XVII	173
Part Three – XVIII	179
Part Three – XIX	183
Part Three – XX	191
Acknowledgements	195

All positive religion rests on an enormous simplification of the manifold and wildly engulfing forces that invade us; it is the subduing of the fullness of existence. All myth, in contrast, is the expression of the fullness of existence, its image, its sign; it drinks incessantly from the gushing foundations of life. Hence religion fights myth where it cannot absorb and incorporate it. It is strange and wonderful to observe in this battle religion ever again wins the apparent victory, myth ever again wins the real one. The prophets struggled through the word against the multiplicity of the people's impulses, but in their visions lives the ecstatic fantasy of the Jews which makes them poets of myth without their knowing it. The Essenes wished to attain the goal of the prophets through a simplification of the forms of life, and from them was born that circle of men that supported the great Nazarene and created his legend, the greatest triumph of myth. (Martin Buber)

Jenny Koralek

PART ONE – ELIZABETH
I

'I say: had Mary not borne God in spiritual fashion first, he never had been born of her in the flesh.'
(Meister Eckhart)

She's gone.

Maryam.

My cousin.

Maryam.

    She in whom the unutterable name dwelt in every cell, in every breath, and in whose womb the Word became flesh and dwelt among us ...
    Never again will I see her lovely face, the compassion in her deep dark eyes, the brave, tender mouth, her gravity as she pondered on hard sayings, her endurance in front of unspeakable horrors, the lines from smiling, the lines from sorrowing; never again absorb her stillness as we worked at silent prayer, watch her attentive way with a spindle, the enfolding curve of her arm, light round the shoulder of a weeping child; never again feel the firm clasp of her hands in mine as she leaned to kiss me; never again watch her face bright with joy at the sight of the lilies of the field, or of a lamb, new-born, struggling to stand but falling again, or a butterfly arrayed in colours like Solomon in all his glory.
    Maryam, Maryam, sweet cousin, sweet mother.

I thought I could not love her more until they killed my son.

Yes, I was the first to undergo that piercing, tearing, shredding of the womb which is the pain of child-losing, harder even than the pangs of child-bearing.

I will never forget how she took me into her bed for many nights, trying to warm me — for I was so cold — cold as a winter night in Jerusalem, though it was high summer, never forget this first experience of the immensity of her love as she held me through my weeping, silent or loud; her tears blending with mine, her strong hands tenderly kneading my muscles, tight in my refusal to acknowledge the murder of my Jochanan.

But also never will I forget her, the woman of sorrows, acquainted with grief, and her control, as she stood hour after hour at the foot of the cross, and her entirely human deep swoon as they took Him down from it as gently as they could.

PART ONE – II

'In truth, in truth I say unto you that among those born of women there has never risen a greater man than Jochanan'

No, she's gone.

I saw her go.

He came for her Himself.

In a vision I saw them.

    A vision — vouchsafed to me at last, Elizabeth, the cousin, and mother of the cousin, Jochanan, my son, the man sent from God, who considered himself not worthy to undo the straps of His sandals, and who would make the way straight for Him, baptize Him with water and ... die, murdered, his head served up on a silver dish ... upon a platter.

    I can hear my outrage, my anguish, but it is not as if I had not known what was ahead for me as his mother — they had tried to prepare me, tell me, when they <u>told</u> her why she had come into being.

    He came for her Himself and I am left here, and left to die a more ordinary death, I, the witness, like Jochanan my son, whose destiny was not to enter the kingdom of heaven, which was not a kingdom at all, nor a distant, blissful paradise, but a shocking new possibility here and now.

Jenny Koralek

PART ONE – III

'Hail Maryam, full of grace, the Lord is with thee ...'

But I must not forget. There are many who do not know the story, so I will begin at the beginning.

I was telling you about Maryam ...

We were cousins, Maryam and I.

Maryam and Elizabeth, the cousins who became sisters in the house of Bethanehyeh — that special place of preparation just where the mountains begin, above the Sea of Galilee ...

We were cousins, distant, but cousins nevertheless, and I was the elder by seven years, and seven years wife to Zacharias, my priestly Zacharias, when Maryam married that good man, the carpenter, Joseph of Nazareth. But we did not know one another well until we met in that sacred enclosure.

We did not know one another well, not only because we lived quite far from one another, but because, I came to think, my parents felt a certain awe of Maryam's parents and the extraordinary things that had happened to them. Perhaps, too, they had felt guilty that they had their daughter at home with them while, keeping their promise, Maryam's parents were parted from their beloved daughter by the time she was three ...

But I said I would begin at the beginning.

Maryam was the daughter of Hannah and Joachim.

Like Sara and Abram before them they had been married long yet remained childless.

They were rich; Joachim gave far more than the required tenth of his wealth to the community and the Temple — rich, but sorrowing with an ache, an emptiness which grew yearly harder to bear — an ache, an emptiness I too was to know with my husband, Zacharias.

Rich, but childless, until they became serious about prayer ...

Hannah herself told me most of the story. Told me how it all came to pass. Sometimes we sewed together or carded wool in that place of preparation I will soon tell you about. In the rhythmic intimacy of that work she would begin to speak — tell me a part here, a part there, as if piecing together her own patchwork memory of how it all came to pass ...

"Together at first, we tried to open ourselves to a different way of praying ..."

"A different way of praying?" I interrupted. "Tell me. Tell me what that would be. All I know, all I practise are the daily blessings and supplications taught to me by my mother. Is that not, then, sufficient?"

Hannah smiled.

"Yes, indeed, it is a necessary beginning, a good foundation. You have not been here long, but you will learn what I mean for yourself."

"But tell me now!" I begged. "At least give me an idea ..."

"What we learned at our mother's knee," Hannah replied, "may be adequate until I come up against shock, anguish, a terrible sense of being lost, alone, helpless, overwhelmed ..."

I had to admit that none of this had yet been my experience. That I missed my Zacharias was true; that I sometimes felt the demands which I sensed were slowly being made of me increasing in their severity, but in all honesty I could not own to knowing anguish. I could not know then as we talked that by the time my son was grown, imprisoned, beheaded, how often I would fall on my knees in gratitude that during those days at Bethanehyeh I had indeed finally, slowly, painfully, learned 'a different way of praying.'

But that day I was impatient, eager, greedy even, to know what Hannah meant.

"So, what then?" I demanded. "What changes once I have known such sufferings?"

"You stop asking. You stop offering your slipping-off-the-tongue blessings and thanking, your almost thoughtless recitals. You yourself have to act, to do something, something for yourself, for no-one can do it for you. You no longer just recite. You <u>open</u>. Intentionally you bring about an opening. You learn to open like the sunflower turning to the sun, and somehow you know that this will do good for you even though you have no idea in what way. You open and you call. You call on ... you no longer know what you call on, but nevertheless you are calling for help. It is a precarious movement, risky. I cannot know what will come of it. It is out of my hands. It is perhaps what is called 'faith'? No longer reciting, I enter in as I would into some sacred space.

"I become still.

"I become silent.

"I put myself under — under I know not what, except that it is above me and very great.

"<u>That</u> is opening. <u>That</u> and that alone is my part, my necessary part.

"That is what we tried, Joachim and I, but however much we tried nothing seemed to shift. Finally we realised that this was something that could not be shared. Besides, we had to admit that our self-pity was still there, so then we decided to separate, to try alone ...

"I felt abandoned and helpless when Joachim went away ... For forty days and forty nights he was away, away in the wilderness, living among the shepherds, surrounded only by silence, only broken by the needy noises of the animals. Watching the way they rounded up their sheep and lambs together, he collected his wandering thoughts, distanced himself a little from them, fasted, fell silent within himself. He remembered Abraham who had been Abram until God breathed his own breath into him, bringing him to new life, re-vivifying him ... Abraham, who entertained angels unawares and killed the tender calf for them and had Sarah bake fresh bread for them and brought them milk and curds beneath the shade of the great terebinth trees on the plains of Mamre's land ...

"During those forty days and forty nights I went into a kind of double mourning — a widow and a childless one. I could not eat, I could not sleep. I neglected my dress, my hair, and barely washed. I am ashamed now when I speak of it. But the greatest shame was the reproach of my servant girl. She came to me one morning, just before the High Holy Day and offered me a beautifully embroidered band for my hair. 'You can't go on like this,' she said. 'You must prepare for the High Holy Day. What will others say and think? Here, take this headband — it is far too grand for the likes of me. Perhaps that will help you to get dressed in a proper way.'

"'How dare you!' I cried. 'How dare you speak to me like that! What are you trying to do to me?' 'Oh lady,' she replied. 'I meant to help you. I have nothing but pity for you in your childless state ...' And she pressed the pretty ribbon into my hand and fled, while I remained there, lamenting, bruised, angry ..."

"I'm not surprised," I interrupted. "She had no right to speak to you like that!"

"No, No!" Hannah insisted. "I was more angry with myself than with her; I thank God she did speak to me like that, for surely He had put those words into her mouth! For suddenly I came to myself - to a quiet, proper sense of myself.

"I went straight to the bath and washed myself and my long, lank hair. I dressed almost as a bride to welcome the High Holy Day and bound my hair with the silken ribbon. Then I walked slowly down to our orchard of orange trees. And there beneath the leaves, dark, black, green, the heavy blossoms filling the warm air, I thought of ..."

"Sarah?" I interrupted.

"Of course," Hannah replied. "First of Sarah - Abraham's wife - who had been Sara until God breathed into her, put new life and reason for living into her - Sarah who laughed and trembled behind the tent flap when she heard the stranger foretell that she would become a mother after all those barren years. Yes, of course she came first into my mind, but then too I had a glimpse, a vision of that other Hannah, mother of Samuel, whom she lent to God as a servant in His temple; Samuel who would become the great prophet ..."

Hannah put down her sewing and stared into the far, far distance.

Then, "Oh!" she whispered. "Oh!"

"What is it? What is it?" I urged, dreading she would not finish her tale because she had remembered some chore she should be attending to elsewhere.

"I've only just *seen*, understood - they - Hannah *lent* her child to God; Isaac was *saved* from sacrifice at the very last minute, but I *gave* my Maryam to the rabbis in the Temple - I *gave* her before she was born -

I *promised* that before she was born ... I gave *her* and *she*, oh, she in her turn will give even more ..."

And great slow tears began to bloodstain the dark red stuff, the sewing in her lap.

"Yes, I know, Elizabeth. Grace, Wisdom - these great attributes with which I am imbued, to which I have been given - are not supposed to be wounded by mortal sorrows - and indeed *they* are not. But my other nature, as Hannah the woman, Hannah, the mother, feels, fears, anticipates her own sufferings and the sufferings which will come upon her daughter."

More great tears were falling onto her sewing.

I felt so unable to enter into her suffering, even though her words - all of them - about a different kind of prayer had seared themselves into my heart like a red-hot soldering iron, I thought it best to turn her mind back to her thoughts of Sarah.

"I do not understand these things," I murmured, "and can only hope that by the time I leave here I will ... But, dear Hannah, you were telling me of how, washed and dressed, you walked upright in your orchard and thought of Sarah?"

"Yes," sighed Hannah, "indeed there I was, wondering if her laugh that day behind the tent flap was as bitter as I knew mine would have been, and I returned to my grieving, staying there with Sarah behind that tent flap - and then suddenly, I sensed myself! That my shoulders were beginning to droop again. My body had taken up its habitual posture of despair, of self-pity. Something made me straighten again and gave me courage. I remember my fingers flying to that bright ribbon. *Take a different path, Hannah*, I told myself and I thought of my Joachim, my beloved - how he had bravely separated himself from me and gone far away into the quiet fields beneath the great sky. I knew how seriously he would be working on his inner self, how hard, how faithfully, how trustingly, he would be trying to align himself with that something above us and so much greater than us. I felt ashamed of myself, of my feeble effort of dressing properly. I found my feet leading me towards the old oak tree at the far end of our orchard and there I sank to the warm earth and leaned my back against the tree's great trunk and allowed myself to feel the sheer pleasure of sitting there like that.

"Gradually I felt my hands uncurl, my spine lose the rigidity of a wrongly imposed discipline. My breathing grew slow and steady, and, when I closed my eyes a light was there – here, she pointed, in the centre of my forehead — a blue light that sometimes ran through all the colours of the rainbow before becoming white and seemingly warm, spreading a glow down and down through my whole body.

"It was as if my grieving fell away, leaving a vibrant emptiness, not, you must understand, an emptiness of dark loss. It was something quite different which I had never experienced before - a completely new kind of *acceptance*. I do not have the least idea how long I must have sat there like that. I have come to think, to believe, even, that I was outside time itself, even more so because, at some point, I became aware of the angel ..."

"The angel?" I whispered. "The angel?"

"Yes," answered Hannah, who, as she told me her story, seemed to be transforming in front of my very eyes. Growing, becoming larger than life and yet without any distortion, but as if the re-telling had restored her to the magnitude of Grace. I was beginning to sense that Maryam had been born to fulfil some mysterious destiny.

"Yes. The angel. I had been sitting there for some while with my eyes closed and then I became aware of a rustling of the leaves of the tree and then I could swear that the lower boughs began to bend their branches down around me, so that I seemed to be in a green bower. There was this slight breeze but nothing strong enough to bend branches. No, it was as if it was coming from the life of the tree itself, as if it wished to embrace me ... And, of course, then I opened my eyes and there ... there was ..."

"An angel, you said. How - how did you know it was an angel?"

"I do not know what else to call it," said Hannah. "It was certainly more a presence than a human form ... or else a stranger from some very far land .... Light was all around it and not from our bright sun ... No, it was its own light and the all of it was smiling — it seemed to be smiling at <u>me</u> and wishing me well ..."

"Were you afraid?" I asked.

Hannah did not reply at once.

"No," she said. "No, I was not frightened. I seemed to be enveloped in goodness, embraced by well-wishing."

"Did — did it speak to you?" I asked softly.

"Oh yes," said Hannah. "Twice I heard *Hannah, Hannah* and I heard my answer though so soft and low I was not sure I had spoken out loud. 'Here am I! Here am I!' And I had leapt to my feet.

"I will never know if I heard all of what was being told to me, but, 'Your suffering has been great.' That is what I heard. 'Your suffering has been great ... Your emptying had to be complete before you could give birth to a child ...'

"Of course I could not speak, but fell to my knees again and pressed my forehead to the ground. I felt a huge warmth and myself being raised up, my hands taken so that I was standing face to face with ... this great presence, this angel ... I gasped, and heard the voice of it: 'Yes, Hannah, go now to the gate of the city, the Golden Gate and there you will find your Joachim, who, as I speak, is running in answer to a dream towards you from those distant pastures. Go now to meet him. Go home together. Go in to your chamber. I tell you now that you are blessed. Your womb will bear a new life full of the grace that your name carries with it ...'

"By now I was weeping and once more falling to my knees I cried out, 'My soul doth magnify the Lord and I vow to thee here and now as this your messenger is my witness that this child promised to me will be at thy service all its days ...'

"If an angel could smile it was then that I sensed a patient amusement, for the voice said: 'This has been known since before you and Joachim were born.' I felt foolish, but again a great heat spread through me. I understood that Joachim and I were to serve some much higher purpose in conceiving a child. From this great presence there in front of me I was being given the strength to bear it; the child would be ours and yet not ours.

"I bowed my head and, then, I felt as if I was being kissed on the top of my head. It was at that point where sometimes I sense that light I was telling you about, which pierces my skull and enters me from the space between my eyes ..."

"The angel kissed you!"

"I think so," said Hannah, and again I saw the tears roll and drop onto her blood-red sewing.

"You think so?"

I could not hide my envy at the thought of such an experience.

"How could you not remember?"

I cannot believe that I could have asked such a crude question, and I certainly paid for my insensitivity in her reply.

"It is a terrible as well as a wonderful thing to be visited by an angel ... I do not know how anyone could stand it more than once...that light, that rushing sound of a wind in the great wings, that voice unlike a man's or a woman's...as if forming words out of flame. No, do not envy me unless you envy the effect of this visitation, which left me in no doubt that there are far higher forces above and below us and around us than we know...unless perhaps in the greatest moment of need, fear, or abandonment to a certain kind of love ..."

"And then?"

"Suddenly the orchard was emptied of angel energy. The sparrows were twittering again and the air heavy with the scent of orange flowers and I saw a little movement [again] in the leaves as if a wind had just ceased to blow upon them ... And I lifted my skirts and ran, ran like a girl, to the Golden Gate and into the arms of my Joachim and kissed him. We went at once and silently to our house, but our hands so tightly clasped, our bodies touching, our eyes seeking one another, a tear on his cheek, a small smile on my lips ... We shut ourselves in our chamber and loved one another. We did not talk then about what had happened to us both. We were too much in awe of it."

Hannah and I were silent until I felt able to say, "Thank you, Hannah for telling me what you and Joachim suffered in order to give birth to my cousin, Maryam, and for that promise you made and kept. I don't know how you did it."

In my heart I thanked her for not dwelling on the joys of the nine months of the child growing in her womb, the quickening at the fourth month as if some invisible, affectionate creature had patted one softly on the cheek. When at long last my turn came to curve my hands round my growing belly, to feel the child beneath my heart, the child I would discover that for myself: that unconditional love of a mother for the child beneath her heart, the child that I would love even beyond death, the child's or my own, a love quite unlike any other.

"Of course, we in the family heard all those miraculous tales of little Maryam's infancy and early childhood ..."

Hannah laughed.

"There were no miracles. Just the ordinary life of a babe and a little one ... well," she paused, "well, at least for those first short years ... the three years before we took her to the Temple ... Just the anxious first sucklings, the nights where she cried and nothing would comfort her, the careful bathing and drying of plump limbs, the bliss of watching her sleeping, rose-cheeked, long-lashed, little fists unfolding like pink petals, the first steps, the first tumbles, the first words: 'Ma-ma ... Ma ... ma, Pa ... Pa ... ba;' the anxious nights when fever struck; Joachim making a doll; killing a snake come too close; her laughter at the lizards on the sunbaked wall; her delight in the butterflies and the birds; the red cheek as the teeth came through ... Oh no, Elizabeth, there were no miracles! The miracles began when she went into the Temple — and I dare say those are what you heard from your dear Zacharias. For then it was that the angels came to teach her, but not as her teachers taught her. The priests taught her the letters, the prayers, and a little later the women of the Temple taught her how to spin the scarlet and purple threads which adorn the Temple ..."

"And to dance?"

"And to dance, of course, as all our women have danced ..."

"Since the day her namesake, the sister of Moses, that other Maryam, took up her timbrel and danced on the further shore of the Red Sea ..."

"Indeed," agreed Hannah. "I can see her now, that day we took her to the Temple with the other young girls, each carrying a bright lamp, 'so that our child will not turn to us and beg to come home with us,' as Joachim said. It was a joyful sight — all the girls with their lights and the priests singing and welcoming her, knowing she was special, kissing her and leading her to sit upon the altar steps. Not for one moment did she seem sad to be leaving us. It was as if we were all surrounded by a great loving force like a beating of wings that held us all together and would continue to do so — and did so — when we parted."

"But," I insisted, "we heard that the angels even _fed_ her?"

"The angels in silence taught her silence, but a living, vibrant silence which brings about opening, wondering, wordless pondering ... and this silence was all about her as she learned the letters and the prayers and the rituals and even the spinning of the thread ... that was the food they fed her."

And we too fell silent over our wool, until Hannah spoke again, saying, "The angels attended her, and that is what has set her apart from all the others there — they were working on her to create the space, the saturation of her cells, the womb space for her to give birth to the Word made flesh ..."

She paused and looked up and around us — at the beauty of that place, the mountains in the distance, the strong blue sky, the silver green of the olive groves, the flowers in the field.

"And now we are here to help her — you too, my dear Elizabeth, even if you do not yet know the secrets of it all — to help her give a form to the Formless. <u>That</u> is why we are here in this special place."

She began to fold her sewing neatly.

"And now it is time to join the others for the mid-day meal."

PART ONE - IV

'Twice every day they pray, at dawn and at eventide ... that the soul where she is consistory and council chamber to herself pursue the quest for truth ...'

We lived, Maryam and I, for three years in simple dwellings of stone, set among olive groves at the foot of the great mountains, where the streambeds run dry in summertime. The white dusty road below was edged with small vineyards, hung with the dark sweet grapes we shared between us at the end of the day and little straight furrows where we grew the vegetables we ate, the pale yellow of the marrow-flowers, the purple eggplants, the pale-skinned pomegranates, concealing the blood drops of its fleshy seeds, the melons and the bee-hives whose bees fed off the orange flowers.

    For three years we rose just before the sun did, and in that state between sleeping and waking, where forms are nameless and thoughts have not yet stirred, gathered together facing the East to watch the immense rays begin to spread out across the world, emanating from the great red gold globe which will blind anyone who is foolish enough to look it in the face. We would watch the rose-red, blood-gold light touch the dark, hear the first dog howl, the birds begin to sing. Likewise at sunset, at certain times of the year when the moon-half of the sky begins to turn green and silver as the sun is going down, a different kind of twilight from dusk, we always gathered again and attended to the going down of the sun and welcomed the departure of the high heat of noon. At the time of full moon we would wait to see her dance on the tip of the mountain peak. And when a shooting star began to fall across the black sky a great sigh would go up from us all ...

It was a perfect, sacred ground.

A perfect enclosed space within which to offer and so empty ourselves, a place where we worked at the simple tasks, and danced, and sang, and prayed at sunrise and sunset — prayed as I came to understand and experience for myself in the way that Hannah had described to me — trying again and again to make sacred all that we did, from cooking and sweeping, from tilling the earth, grinding our grain, making honey or cheese, from carding wool to seeking the last lost sheep, up to the purest of our hymns, the most appropriate movements of our silent dancing bodies, and our most attentive prayer, all, all with the deep wish that this influence would find its way into the turbulent world and act upon it.

But I am making it sound so easy. No it was not easy; it was never easy; the body revolted again and again <u>and again</u>; it often ached all over; it was often tired, footsore. The weather was either too hot, or too cold. There were terrifying sudden rainless thunderstorms. The mind would chatter away as if a monkey was at its entrance, stealing thoughts indiscriminately; cracking them open like nuts, either eating the kernels or spitting them out. I never got used to the smelly goats and having to drink their smelly milk. There were little snakes and not so little scorpions, but worst of all was a little voice as if from some small creature sitting on my shoulder whispering: 'Not today ... Not today. Your admirable struggle could start tomorrow or even the next day. There's plenty of time ...' Apart from that vicious little voice there was nothing different in my attitude from when I had been at home, but there, of course, all my grumblings and fears poured out automatically. I had not been practising this huge demand for a certain kind of awareness.

It was to be many years before I sensed the existence of an almost tangible substance dwelling in my spinal column which burned the question into me: from where had it come? Could it be the result of the friction between my assent to try to work for consciousness to appear and my frequent refusals to do so? I came to feel it was lodged in my very marrow bone, giving me the capacity to bear unimaginable sorrows, and marvelled that such a force could have come into being from such small daily discomforts.

And most surely, if it was given to me, Elizabeth, to be aware of what was going on deep inside me, most surely that same substance was at work a hundredfold in Maryam?

It was the perfect, enclosed, sacred place for Maryam's own preparation; the perfect, enclosed, sacred space for the women who came to visit us, for the mysterious visitations, quite outside ordinary time, ordinary space, for the making of the womb space within which a new kind of birth could take place ...

But you have heard my voice enough.

Listen now to Maryam.

I begged her to write down what happened there. It took a long time for her to agree.

"But only you can tell it how it was," I said. "It is <u>your</u> story ..."

"No, Elizabeth," she said, "it is <u>the</u> story, but often only heard tell in dreams and then in fragments — or lit up briefly, a page or two, like a room full of familiar objects, by a bright lightning flash ..."

"Set it down," I urged her. "You, Maryam, you, set it down ..."

Jenny Koralek

PART TWO – MARYAM
I

'It had been a Jewish girl who, at the command of the Voice which sounded in her ears, in her heart, along her blood and through the central cells of her body, had uttered everywhere in herself the perfect Tetragrammaton ...'
(Charles Williams in *All Hallows' Eve)*

"Set it down," my cousin Elizabeth begged, not for the first time. "I wish you would set it down now. We are not getting any younger, you and I .... so set it down now ... If you do not tell the story, what do you think they will hear? That you were some simple, ignorant village girl? Unprepared? Tell the story — tell just what a burden was laid on you from the moment of your birth."

"It began long before that," I interrupted. "It began before I was born ..."

And it was then, when I saw Elizabeth's outer shock and sensed her inner astonishment that I agreed to her wish ...

It began before I was born.

And how could I not have been born? Or called into being, since the need once again was very great — the need for love to manifest again.

How could I not then be born? Take on a form? Become the container of the uncontainable ... Become the consenting vessel for the entrance into matter of the 'new Adam', the entrance into matter of the <u>Breath</u>, of the spirit, of yHvH as breath, which was to animate man and woman in a new way.

Jenny Koralek

I was in a place of light and there was the sound of water falling ... there was laughter and delight in the air, but with a foundation of gravity, respect, intention. A great benevolence, a goodness, a love seemed to be there above me. I saw cherubim and seraphim ... then all this faded and a sound murmured into me, subtle, beneficent, or was it a breath breathed into me, almost, but not quite, indefinable; which flowed into me from the top of my head to the soles of my feet, poured and spread through my blood into my very marrow. "yHvH ... YHVH ... YAHWEH," I heard. Then "EHYEH ASHER EHYEH: I am here, always present," and a voice told me, "It is time for the energies to descend once more ... for the spark to fly downwards once more ... for formlessness to take on form once more ... for a special child to be born from the pure longings of a man and a woman once more ... a special child who, in her turn, wholly virgin, that is, void of all images, of all that hinders, empty as she was when she did not exist, will give birth to another special child ..."

And then I was given to a name, but at once told: "This name does not belong to you; you belong to this name, to the service of this name."

I was given to the Hebrew name M A R Y A M [**mem, resh, yod, final mem**].

"Be guided by the meaning of the name," I was told. "Be guided by the letters of the name. Study them. No meaning has been forced into the letter. No, the letter comes into being from the meaning." So I drew them in the air before me:

mem ... which begins with the little hook of **yod**, first letter of the Unsayable, the Tetragrammaton, before it curves protectively to encircle the earth with the highest, finest atoms of consciousness, a loving arm, leaving space within itself to gather up that fine matter ... **mem** as matrix ... **M** ... **mother** ... **mother** ... **mother**.

Next comes **resh** ... the necessary movement without which nothing can be achieved ... **resh** whose shape, as I draw it, shows that the first impulse comes down from above, to give life, to radiate life ever outwards like a holy stone thrown from a height into the vast waters ... endlessly rippling its effect outwards, outwards ... **R**.

Now **yod**, the little hook from above, which sparks off the unutterable **Yod Hay Vav Hay** that indispensable "yes" — without which nothing comes into life ... **Y** ... and I saw that all the letters of the name to which I had been given contain the little active spark of **yod** ...

Last comes the **final mem**, the little hook of **yod** again joined to **mem** now complete as a square, a whole, a treasure, a harvest gathered in ... **M..M A R Y A M**.

"Yes," came the response when I offered my joyful understanding of each of these letters, but the meaning of the whole is its opposite. The meaning of the whole is revolt, rebellion, disobedience, and from that will flow sorrow, grief, bitterness, lamentation ...

All these words were hardly uttered, barely formed, shimmering with potential, asking tenderly, yet rigorously for the best possible understanding ...

I trembled.

"What," I murmured, "is the revolt, the disobedience contained in the meaning of the name to which I belong?"

"This is a new kind of revolt or disobedience which will allow something matchless in light and grace and meaning and joy to be born ... There have been others before you, precursors, prophets, special children, but until now they have all served the familiar, the established level of the relationship between above and below — served it well, creating a firm foundation for your appearance, which is intended to lift that relationship higher, to serve as a sampler for what is wished for men and women on that earth — that they too may give birth to themselves ..."

I wished I could speak but could not.

"But now you have understood that you belong to the name, that the name does not belong to you, you will understand that this is not yet your assertion of self, but a bowing to the mysteries of these seeming contradictions ... You said the letters spoke to you first and foremost as mother. But you are to be *virgin* mother ..."

"*Virgin* mother?" I must have spoken aloud, for the shimmering sound grew less faint, and I heard very clearly indeed. "Only where opposites meet can new life come into being, and the new life that will be born out of your form will be intentional, formed to create a movement upwards, to hold firmly that ladder which Jacob dreamt he saw stretching between heaven and earth ..."

"Will I remember this once I am born?" I heard myself ask.

And now stronger voices were there, speaking in turn.

"You will remember because we are helping you now to absorb the degree of surrender, the active passivity which will be demanded of you ..."

"We can see by the posture of your entire being that you assent to these mysteries ..."

"And this, child," came a particularly sweet voice, "is awe and love and the beginning of wisdom ..."

"We acknowledge that your being weeps ..."

"But also rejoices ..."

And then I heard tongues I did not know then were the tongues of the world I was soon to be born into ... fragments which must have found their way into my bloodstream, my marrow, all my cells ... *"Magnificat anima mea Dominum ... My soul doth magnify the lord; Exsultavit spiritus meus; qui fecit mihi magna ... for he that is mighty hath done to me great things ...; the lowliness of his handmaiden ...; car le Tout-Puissant a fait pour moi de grandes choses ...; he, remembering his mercy hath holpen his servant Israel ...; a sword shall pierce through my own soul also; Salve Regina ... o clemens, o dulcis virgo ... mater dolorosa ...; Holy mother ... tender mother ..."*

And now a sound came out of me, a sound of terror ...

"You will be helped," I heard.

"By whom?" I whispered.

"Why, by your own mother ... who else? For you will be the child of Hannah, of grace itself ..."

And then I fell into a deep sleep ... the sleep of birth, but from a little child — whenever I looked into my mother's eyes — some kind of remembering passed between us, as if in that exchange we could both see back to Eva, the long, long line of birth-giving women, the long, long line of existence. My mother was dear and pleasing to me, and I saw that I was dear and pleasing to her. I saw that she was favoured and that the favour shone on me. I saw that she was virtuous and that the virtue fell on me. I saw that the outward becomingness of her conduct was a reflection of her deep inner becomingness and that too pierced me. I found favour in her look, the kindness that was in it — the good feeling of true kinship.

I should tell you here at once that just as I had been promised, she indeed helped me, that without her there would have been no 'preparation', no 'special education' for the role — for I cannot call it <u>my</u> role.

Jenny Koralek

PART TWO - II

On our last evening in Bethanehyeh, we, Elizabeth and I, were sitting outside in the warm dark and the bright starlight waiting to be eclipsed by the fast rising full moon ...

My beloved mother had retired to her simple room.

Yet we could not sleep, still could not quite believe what had come to pass over the past days — or was it hours or was it weeks? Or had it been in quite some other kind of time ... not of the ordinary world ... the time of the house of "I AM"?

Although we knew our visitors had returned (fading, dissolving before our eyes) to wherever they had come from, I know that like me Elizabeth was straining slightly in the starry dark for a soft sigh, a muted footstep, hoping even they would join us once more in that almond shape, womb shape, that mysterious *mandorla* which we had all made together ...

And when the full moon showed herself, poised on the top of the mountain-shape like a great ball which might begin at any moment to spin, and when her rays lit up the night so that we could have read a book open on our knees, I do not know which of us wished, hoped more for a last sight or a new sight of those women who had become our sisters, whichever world we or they might inhabit at any given moment ...

Hannah, my mother, had called the first meeting when she knew I was ready.

And all at once there were signs, signs that I was ready.

First there came a moment of formlessness ...

Before dawn.

The very landscape — turned from its lovely form — dark mountains close by, higher ones further off, which I knew would turn golden later in the day — the clusters of shrubs, olives, cypress, the occasional lime or apricot, the lavender clumps, the round field full of sunflowers — all, for a moment out of time, gone ...

Instead, as I went outside from the simple sleeping place — total silence, total; heavy mist, turning white in the beginning hint of light — my mind empty of everything — as near to no-thing-ness as I, an ordinary woman, am ever likely to be ...

Of course it did not last more than a few seconds and now I am glad it did not. I love the form. I love the formlessness. I love to live coming and going between the two ...

And then, that same morning, I saw the white rainbow.

It did not last long, the white rainbow. Yes, white and I was not the only one who saw it. There had been rain the night before, heavy for that part of the world and heavy for that time of year, and following a very hot day ...

As usual we had risen at dawn into that full silence — the dogs never barked till the sun began to rise; the crows never left their roosts, cawing low over the fields, till the sun began to rise.

But that morning there was so much thick white mist we could hardly say we had seen the sun rise, just catching the hints of pink and gold — haze more than rays — through the cloud ...

Nevertheless, we stayed there as always, in prayer.

Prayer ... but not that of habitual repetition, not that of a self-interested supplication to a wrathful or a benevolent God, but something much more difficult, uncertain, the contact easily lost, the contact with an intent, an intended inward listening, a turning upwards, a going against the down-pourings of manifested life, towards ... silence ... silence ... silence ... and a new kind of consciousness, a new experience of reality, holy wholeness, waiting upon a sharing of the possibility, the fact of infinite existence ...

In this kind of prayer where I am vulnerable, open, at risk; where each word is taken in like a food, something is realised while the words are being spoken, in the very act of prayer itself ... so it can never be the same, never ...

And the prayer is *the* prayer which Moses brought, understanding that a form is necessary for us to pass beyond into the formlessness, the endlessness of silence.

"*Shema, Ish-ra-el; Hear, O Israel,*" we said then, and still say every day, listening to the call, listening our way towards the silence of yHvH ... Ish-ra-el, struggling upwards to the Silence ... love yHvH with the all of you .... Silence ...

And only when we finally turned away, still empty, still silent, did we see the white rainbow ...

Some rare natural combining of moisture, heat, light, I don't know, but for me it was a sign — all the colours of the rainbow coming together in one colour, all the different strands coming together to a unity — I stared into the whiteness and knew I had to obey the sign, step over a new threshold, open to I knew not what, obey the call I had heard for so long, obey it without yet understanding ... this call coming it seemed from both within me and from without, this call I had begun to accept that I did not understand, need not even understand, but remain open to receive, in silence, to bear, to carry, to suffer, to ponder ...

And then it faded. As the heat of the sun increased, it evaporated and disappeared.

And Hannah, my mother, knew that at daybreak and at sunrise there had been signs.

She knew then I was ready to make the *mandorla*, the almond shape, ready to meet the others.

After the white rainbow the day began to unfold like any other. Till noon I worked with the others at all the simple, necessary tasks — the milking of the goats, the sweeping, the washing, the baking of bread, the preparing of food from plants and fruits grown in our gardens and groves. In the afternoon, in the coolest room of the house, we had been studying the meaning of our Hebrew letters, the very foundation of the way we pray, but on this day, after the mid-day meal, Hannah, my mother, sent for my cousin Elizabeth and me. "I want you both to go and rest," she said. "We will have visitors later — a company of women. They come to help you, Maryam," she added so gravely, so mysteriously I dared not ask her what she meant. She had not said they were also to help Elizabeth. Hannah saw that my gaze was on my dear cousin's face. "I am glad you love Elizabeth. By coming here she has given up much for you. You will need each other very much from this day on in order to understand better what is to be shown ..."

We did as we were told and went to rest. Of course we were both tempted to wonder out loud what Hannah had meant, and who the company of women might be, but each time we looked at each other silence prevailed.

But when the day began to cool and the sun to sink rose gold, my mother came for us and led us to a large space in the middle of the most ancient olive grove and told us to sit down upon the warm red earth.

A little breeze began crackling the silvery leaves and dropping every now and then an olive to the ground.

And then great, quiet figures appeared in among the thick, twisted trunks. Suddenly they were there like ghosts, yet not ghostly, but substantial — and tall. Tall, yet not towering, not towering and yet we had to look up to them in order to meet their gaze. By now my mother was moving forward with arms outstretched in greeting and we, of course, we were on our feet.

"The mothers," said Hannah quietly ... "Mothers," she repeated, "sisters, daughters ... Eva ..." She murmured each name in turn and took them by the hand one by one and signalled for us to come forward ... "Sarah, Rebekah, Leah and Rachel; Ruth, Miriam the prophetess, and the daughters of Job — Keziah, Jemima and Kerenheppuch ..."

You would think we would have fainted away with terror at such a visitation, but it was as if there was a spell upon the place, or as if we had stepped into a strong dream ...

I had leapt to my feet, my heart leaping too and, to this day I could not tell you why, but I ran to them one after the other and embraced them, but as a desperate child embraces its mother when it needs comforting ... it was as if suddenly I knew my joy and my doom, yet nothing had been said, nothing explained ... Elizabeth too had jumped up, but she just touched their wrists or the sleeves of their robes in a polite and welcoming gesture ... How to describe the appearance of these ten figures? They all allowed me to embrace them, but did not all return the embrace, but rather resisted it — all, that is, except Eva, who put her arms round me, held me briefly, murmured something too low for me to hear and kissed me on the forehead. How indeed to describe them, the sense they gave out of immensity, the suffering and joy in their faces, neither young nor old, yet both young and old, the way their bodies moved, a flowing verticality, not bowed or bent, not stiff; girlish, yet matronly: Eva, Rebekah and Rachel sensual and very, very beautiful; Leah plainer but with a bloom on her like a luscious, ripe fruit, her eyes large and soft, often downcast. And Sarah, striking, tall, silver-haired, matriarch of matriarchs. Miriam, handsome with an independent glint in her eyes and Ruth, slighter than the others, her gentleness concealing the courage and determination she most surely had.

How too to describe the robes they wore? After this long time it is hard to remember the details, but assuredly all the colours of the rainbow were there. I do remember the wives of Jacob were decked out in glorious reds and yellows, bejewelled with heavy gold bangles, necklaces, ear-rings. Ruth, I recall, wore some duller colour — I see her still as a little brown bird. Miriam — I think I was frightened of Miriam; she seemed more severe than the others. Miriam wore white with a belt of bronze. As for the daughters of Job, in their plain dresses of madder rose, the colour faded as if from much wearing, much washing, they looked as if they had just put down their brooms and taken off their aprons.

And Eva? The mother of all living wore green, matching her green eyes and setting off her thick coppery hair.

They sank to the ground and we followed after them, my mother indicating I should face her with Eva and Elizabeth on each side of me. The *mandorla* shape, the almond shape, the vaginal shape was formed by all our bodies, as if all knew the shape needed.

Hannah did not have to ask for silence. It fell upon us naturally.

And then Eva spoke.

Jenny Koralek

PART TWO - III

'To know the stages of the creative process is also to know the stages of one's own return to the root of all existence.'
(Gershon Scholem)

"When the apple was eaten," she told us, "I did not exist. I came later. By the time I appeared the apple had been eaten."

Now this shocked me. This was not how it had been told. Eva carried all the blame. That is what I had heard.

"From the highest world," Eva continued, "the Lord God emanates, sends out his thought. And I paid, we paid for a thought — for God's thought, the Lord God's thought. The Lord God in his One-ness, his Absoluteness, in his Formlessness created a second world, the world of his thought. The thought may have been that he was tired of being unmanifest. And then came the world of his heart. He may have had a wish, a desire to make, to create, to pour out and down the opposites, knowing that the friction between joy and sorrow is like the sand in the shell which can bring forth a jewel. Thus forms began to take shape, but these first were of particles of such a shimmering intensity they were still far, far from the Adam and Eva whose story has come down to the world, as if it was the beginning and not the end of the Lord God's action, this bringing of this world, our world, a fourth world, into existence.

Out of those first shimmering particles he made male and female, but as one. He breathed into this one-ness and it became a living creature. Then he saw that nothing would happen; there must be two. So he put to sleep the living being he had breathed into, male and female created together, and he took a rib and from that rib he drew out and made the wo-man, the intuitive wo-man, who would 'allow', 'bring about' the eating of the apple, but no. It was not I, Eva, who was given to this name, 'mother of all living,' just before we crossed the threshold out of Eden into the harsh world. No, it was not I; it was the wo-man answering to the life force in the form of a serpent twined about the tree. And no, it was not a creeping, slithering, fearsome serpent, but a force, a great vertical force, coiling round the trunk, rustling the leaves, pulsating, tongue flickering, matter itself rising up to meet the offerings pouring down from above, offering the fruit to tempt that God-sent energy knowing the price to be paid would be to be cast down in horizontal form, obliged to run along the ground and enmity put between it and the children of the earth until ..."

She paused, faltered.

"Until?" I urged.

"Until Moses bade it rise up again against the plague in the desert and ..."

"And?"

"And another time will come ... and you will be there to see it ... the time when a cross will be formed of that horizontal, that vertical, and they shall be joined forever ... thanks ... to ..."

Here she glanced at Hannah, my mother, as if asking for permission to continue.

"Thanks to ... your child ..."

She must have seen from my face that I was astonished, surprised by terror and incomprehension.

Again she looked at my mother and something seemed to pass between them, which I caught sight of in a flash — a nod, a fluttering of eyelids, a look of accord, sorrow, acquiescence ...

For then Eva continued, "Has no-one told you?"

"Told me what?" I whispered.

Eva did not answer immediately. She seemed to be gathering herself, filling herself with a formidable presence of severity and love.

Then, "Time has no place here," she said to me quietly. "We are equals as women of sorrow and acquainted with grief ... sisters ... as surely as if we had eaten daily at the same table, played together, shared the same bed since we were born, but above all we are equals because we are mothers — I, mother of all living; you, mother of all dying ... of emptying, of selflessness, of no-thing-ness, transcender of ego, whole ... virgin ...

"I asked you: Has no-one told you? You are to be mother — mother — do you understand? You are to bear the child, the Word made flesh ... and, finally ... you are to be..."

Her voice now was so low I was not sure if I heard right, "you are to be daughter of your own son ..."

Her words were incomprehensible and yet, and yet I understood mysteriously that this was my first test — for what I did not know ... my first degree of pain ... as if she was taking me by the hand through fire and burning me with her knowledge.

"I came into being," she continued, "I came into being to assist the falling into form ... I bore the burden — the result of the Lord God's intentional sleep, intentional self-forgetting ... I bore the burden of the division into two-ness ... I bore the division of that united male and female ... and I have also had to bear the burden put upon me by the world for having plucked the apple, for the shared eating of the apple ...

"But I was not given a form, not given to a name until we were stepping over the threshold out of Eden and into this harsh world."

"'Eva,' said the man, Adam, 'you are Eva: **Hay Vav Hay**, mother of all living,' and he drew me to him in a fierce, lustful embrace to which I responded in that same way, and from that fierce, lustful embrace my son, Cain was born, strong and noisy — out of the shock of falling into form, a refusal of the exile, the descent, a kind of anger and bitterness for which there would be payment."

She paused. "My poor Cain — a cruel role he was to play, for his brother Abel was conceived when we had grown quieter, sadder, seeking to learn how to live in this lower world ...

"Abel — a little babe, a gentle boy — in my heart I knew he was not destined to live long — that it would be a fleeting life, like a vapour which disappears in the heat of the day. Cain killed him, you see. Yes, Cain killed him, because the Lord God preferred Abel's offering of a lamb over Cain's sheaf of wheat ... Killed him; spilled his blood upon the ground and tried to hide himself away. But the Lord God saw him and said, 'Where is Abel?' and Cain answered, 'How should I know? Am I my brother's keeper?' 'Indeed you are,' said the Lord God. 'His blood seeps into the earth. You must pay for this murder — it is your role, your fate. You cannot escape it. It has been lurking, waiting for you by the tent flap since the day you were born. Man has to suffer his way from his present picture of me. I do not want offerings of wheat. I do not want burnt offerings of sheep either. I am trying to lead man within — to seek me within ... to know directly that the Whole on High is not a superior form of himself looking down upon him, dispensing judgement, punishment, needing to be placated, propitiated, but a great energy, a great force longing for hearts and minds open to receive it; and this will take time, much time and may never be understood, or only by a few. It will be a long, long story and your part is on the first page but one and a hard part — the part of the triad which pushes the story on, for there will be a third brother, but you — you will wander the world and men will want to kill you for what you have done to your brother. But see, I will set this mark on your forehead by which they will know not to lay a hand on you, but to leave you alone ...'

"And so," said Eva, " he left us and went far away in his wanderings. We never saw him again, but learnt that he had built a city and married and fathered many fierce, warring sons, and that he and they were feared by everyone and so left isolated and unopposed.

"At last, later, much later, at long last, Adam and I turned to each other in tenderness and love and I conceived and gave birth to this third son, Seth, who loved his father and mother, who took upon himself to begin the redemption of this first family of man and therefore of all its descendants; who laboured long and hard in the fields, who at daybreak and twilight contemplated within himself what the Lord God might have meant that he did not want burnt offerings be they lambs or rams, nor offerings from the field be they ears of wheat or flowers; Seth, who seemed to sense that the kingdom of the Lord was some hidden possibility for man to connect with an awareness of the Whole; that the kingdom of heaven came about when through stillness, silence and contemplation his form, he would tell me, felt as if it were dissolving and blending with light and joy; so strongly did Seth experience some intimation of a new way of understanding that he was heard to murmur more and more often a kind of breathed naming of the Lord God's true meaning. 'YaHweH,' he would breathe softly: 'Yahweh' [**yod, hey, vav, hey**] — 'Here am I!'"

Eva was looking straight at me — at me, so must have seen my eyes widen, heard my gasp, seen me tremble. I looked deep into her eyes. *She knows*, I thought, *she knows I too have experienced this interior piercing, breathed this breath.*

But Eva had not finished.

"When we came into form as we stumbled out of Eden, the heat from the angel's powerful wings fanning the searing heat from its flaming swords, Adam found he was holding on to a piece of the tree, that sacred tree of life. He fashioned a staff from it upon which, as he grew older and older, he leaned more and more often. This same staff became the very rod of Moses which terrified the Pharaoh when it turned into a snake; the selfsame rod with which Moses divided the waters of the Red Sea. This was the rod upon which the brazen serpent suspended itself, so that all who looked up at it were healed of their fiery snake-bites; it was from that same staff of Adam's that Moses struck the rock in that fearsome, endless wilderness so that endless fresh and cooling water flowed into the parched mouths of the wretched children of Israel. It became a beam in Solomon's great temple and one day, one day — soon now — it will find its way to Golgotha, unhappy Golgotha, the place of skulls, of the dead, where it will form the vertical rod of a cross on which a man will indeed die in order to be born anew ..."

Her words had been coming more and more fragmented, halting, heavy, and again she was looking entirely, only at me.

"Yes," she said tenderly, "and you, Maryam, you, you will be there to see it ..."

She paused, and I was glad of it, but it was not long before she spoke again:

"As I came into being to assist the falling, falling, falling into form, so you came into being to assist in the rising, the ascent, the return — for this is man's task, woman's task — to assist the return to formlessness, which is oneness; neither angels, archangels, giants, dwarfs nor demons can do this — only those who dwell inbetween heaven and earth. But the men and women of earth need evidence — they believe nothing they cannot see with their eyes, touch with their fingers ..."

She spoke calmly, slowly, quietly, kindly even, as her ever more mysterious words fell on me like the chill of our bitter winter. But I also sensed a great relief in her voice, as if each word, each phrase was a lessening of some great burden she had been carrying — for how long?

How long? How long? Overwhelmed by this encounter outside time, words whirling, an only half realised inkling of how all she was saying might have something to do with me, I could not formulate a question, let alone speak; I found I was standing up, dumb like an animal bound for slaughter ...

And then ....

PART TWO - IV

"Do not put too much sorrow on her shoulders," came the voice of the oldest among us: Sarah.

"For she will also know joy — the greatest, as I should know — the joy of giving birth. For however different from the rest of ours will be the manner of her conceiving — a mystery, yes, indeed a great mystery — the giving of birth will be the same as for any other woman — long, hard and with pain ... unimaginable before the time comes and, strangely, soon forgotten ...

"I am the only one among us here who has some understanding of the experience of the sacrifice she will be called upon to make ..."

She paused and looked round at the other women one by one before her compassionate gaze again rested upon me.

And she seemed to fall into a reverie.

I think we all felt she had more to say, so we waited in patient silence, our bodies still, the breeze tapping at the dry olive leaves.

A smile flitted across her face as she began once more to speak.

"That day ... behind the tent flap! How I laughed. There we were, long since encamped on the plains of our friend Mamre's lands where the only shade came from one huge old terebinth tree, great tree with holy powers, whose leaves and boughs would bend earthwards should a sleep-laden, sin-laden person lean against its trunk; great tree whose branches and leaves would curve upwards when a man of goodness sheltered there from the heat of the day. I should have known! I should have guessed! For had I not seen my Abraham put these strangers to the test? Had I not seen how the branches almost flung themselves upwards like the arms of a rejoicing dancer; had I not seen the mysterious breeze which blew only through the tree, making the leaves almost ring out like happy little bells and seemed to set the leaves a-whispering 'Holy, holy, holy ...'

"How I laughed when I heard one of three guests tell my Abraham that I would have a child, a son ... How quickly I stopped laughing when I was reproached with such sternness by the tall straight stranger with the dark fire-filled eyes. It was then that I shivered and wondered to myself, *Who are these fine men with their grave faces, their presence-filled demeanour, so light and quick on their feet which never seemed quite to touch the ground? And why had my Abraham greeted that tallest one as 'My Lord'? Whose messengers were they? Were we unknowingly entertaining <u>angels</u>?*

"'Why did you laugh?' he asked gravely.

"I was frightened, so frightened that I lied.

"'I did not laugh, my Lord, I mumbled.'

"And he smiled, more in sorrow than in anger.

"'Oh but yes, Sarah, you did,' he replied.

"He smiled and with a look which pierced my heart.

"So I bowed my head, and nodded, 'Yes, Lord, I did ...'

"'You should have known,' the stranger admonished, 'when I (yes, he said "I" — to this day I swear he said "I") when I changed your name from Sarai to Sarah. You should have known that you were being lifted up ..."'

For a long while Sarah paused, and then continued:

"There is something I have to confess here. I never really felt I deserved my name change, and indeed often supposed that the great sorrow, so equal to my great joy from the birth of my son, Isaac, was the payment for my earlier dark conduct towards Hagar, my maidservant.

"In the long years of my childless state I was blind to Abraham's sorrow until I at last saw it was every much as great as my own. In a moment overflowing with my love for him I gave him Hagar, my servant.

"But my pleasure in my generous act was short-lived. I was exceedingly jealous. Hagar, when she found herself very soon pregnant, was quite unable to prevent herself from gloating over me. Her manner toward me grew daily more disrespectful. When I complained to Abraham he said, 'She's <u>your</u> servant; you must decide what to do about her.'

"My heart hardened; I sent her away — out into the desert. Looking back now, I don't know how I could have done such a thing, but I did. Thank God, she came back the next day. Only years later did she tell me what happened; that she was resting by a well when she seemed to have a vision, heard a voice urging her to return to me and behave to me as she always had; that the child she was carrying would be a great and powerful man ...

"If the story had ended there all would have been well — for I imagined then that if the child was a boy, and I had no son, he would indeed become great as his father was, and that I would have to accept that. But then I learned that I too was to have a child, and with the birth of Isaac I forgave and forgot, until the child born to Hagar, whom she had named Ishmael, began to treat me with disrespect.

"I complained so bitterly and frequently that in the end, with great reluctance, for he loved us all, Abraham sent Ishmael and Hagar into the cruel desert with only one water bag and a little bread.

"This time Hagar did not return. Many years later we began to hear tales of a great archer who had married a woman from Egypt, had much land and many sons. It was Ishmael. I felt a great weight lift from Abraham's heart and I confess from mine too.

"But my shame aroused my feelings of guilt and inadequacy as I listened to the words of this grave, stern stranger. 'You should have known when I changed your name from Sarai to Sarah that you were being lifted up so you could set in motion a cycle of women made fruitful for a purpose: to give birth to sons who will be offered in sacrifice, or sacrifice themselves. The sacrifice is not for a cruel, senseless meaning but to show that what has to be given up for unity to be achieved, for union with me, is that to which man or woman is most attached. Nothing less will do ...'

"He broke off. At last. I could not have borne to hear another word, but then he came closer, and, fixing me with a powerful gaze, murmured, 'There will be more. When your child is born I will return.'

"Then he left me, moving lightly, soundlessly towards his companions, and the three of them seemed to fade away and blend with the mirage shimmering over the desert ...

"And when they had left Abraham came in to me and we loved one another with that heightened glowing, urgent way, which comes about when all else has been ordered, balanced, served, listened to in a very vibrant way."

Now Sarah paused and seemed in the dusk to have the face of a much younger woman, relaxed, fulfilled, satiated, content.

We remained silent until she began to speak again.

"Just as he had promised, the stranger lord appeared to me when my child, Isaac, was not yet one day old.

"He bent over the baby, and at first I thought he wanted a closer look at the miraculous child, but, turning to me again, he said, 'Look on him, mother, as if each day were his last.'

"The voice sent such a chill through me that I started up, pulling the baby off the nipple so suddenly that of course he set up an angry and a frightened wail.

"By the time I had turned from settling him again the stranger had gone.

"*'Look at him, mother, as if each day were his last.'*

"The words were to haunt me and of course I obeyed them, which was not difficult for the child was the light of my Life, the treasure of treasures, but as year after year passed and we lived through the joys and anxieties known to all families, I forgot the dark warning.

"I only understood when it was too late ...

"When Abraham for the first time and only time lied to me.

"The very morning after Isaac's thirteenth birthday, Abraham said, 'Isaac, our son, is old enough now to be taught the ways of the Lord — I am taking him to the priests to study for a time.'

"And I sent them away with my blessings, but not before I had kept Isaac by me all night, talking with him, talking mother's talk — of courtesy, of submission to his elders, of the washing of hands, the brushing of teeth, the thanking for food, and in between unable to refrain from kissing my son, my fingers in his thick dark curls ...

"In the early morning I dressed him in a very fine and beautiful garment and a turban of silk. I even pinned a precious stone into the turban.

"'Oh mother! Foolish mother!' he protested gently.

"Little did I know how unsuitable these garments were for the real path he was about to tread; how they would catch and tear on the thorns and thistles on the narrow path that leads to the mountain of Moriah, that sacred centre where Jerusalem now stands: that same sacred centre where the Tree stood whose fruit was plucked and eaten by Adam — and no, not by Eva, but by his own wo-man long ago."

Here Sarah paused and gazed at Eva, who looked back at her in gratitude.

Once again she fell silent, this time for so long we all began to look at her and saw that she was weeping.

"Yes, even now what happened next still makes me weep ...

"When they returned, father and son, the state of Isaac's clothes alone told me that they had been nowhere near the good priests' clean and simple dwelling close by the temple's clean stark stone.

"There were long scratches on Isaac's forehead, arms, legs. But next to the change in my son and Abraham, the shredded silks and the crusted blood were as nothing.

"My son had parted from me a promising, innocent, beautiful boy.

"He had returned a man — remote, severe, and deeply marked by what he had been through.

"He continued to accord me all the respect and courtesy owed to a mother, but I knew that I had lost him. He had left his mother's house. He had even left his father's house."

Here Sarah paused and her gaze, which had seemed focussed on some faraway point, returned to our faces as if she had forgotten our presence there with her.

"Who among you does not know the story of the near sacrifice of Isaac by his father among the boulders and thickets of Mount Moriah?"

"I don't," said Eva.

"It was a test, you see," Sarah continued. "A test of Abraham's faith and understanding — a new understanding of godhead as an alignment from within with a higher, finer consciousness, and conscience; the need for individual commitment; a proper kind of awe. And now Isaac had seen and understood this, he had grown and gone far ahead, prepared to live this understanding and to pass it on.

"I cursed my foolishness. I had known, for a long time, but without wanting to admit it or join him there — ever since that day we entertained those three strangers — that Abraham had been experiencing a new relationship with the Lord God. And now he tried to explain: He had heard a voice which came neither entirely from within nor from without.

"'Abraham! Abraham!'

"And heard himself answer: 'Here am I!'

"'Whom do you love most?'

"'Isaac, my son, my son ...'

"'Then take him, take your son, Isaac, to a place I will show you and prepare to offer him as a sacrifice ...'

"And Abraham obeyed, but knowing that I would prevent him in each and every possible way, and knowing even more that this command would break my heart, would kill me even, my Abraham lied to me, and even encouraged me in my parting fondness, my pride in dressing Isaac up in such unsuitable garments.

"'I was guided the whole way,' Abraham told me, 'and whenever I faltered — and indeed, I promise you, I did falter many times — my heart cracking each time I dared look at the happy, trusting boy at my side, that voice, from within and yet from without, and, I dare say, seemingly from above me, came again: "Abraham! Abraham!" I had to answer it, and always with the same "Here am I!" And when Isaac looked up at me as we came nearer and nearer to the clearing of flat stones, so evidently intended to be <u>the place</u>; when he looked at me and asked, "Where, dear father, where will we find the burnt offering?" it was then that I knew he was uneasy, fearful, because I could not look at him, could no longer look him in the eye. He knew then who was to be the sacrifice, and did not believe me when I said, "the Lord will provide." He glanced at the sharp knife in my belt, which till that moment he had seen me use only to cut away thorns, or slice the fruits and cheese you had prepared for us ... "'And ... then ... then'

"Abraham, between dry sobs, could barely say the words ...

'And then I saw by the way he forced me to look into his eyes — I saw that he understood that it was he ... he was to be the sacrifice. I felt as if I, the father, in the midst of being tested myself, was myself testing my son's love for me. It was the same obedient love which the Lord seemed to be demanding from me. Isaac had even laid his head on the flattest stone when I saw the ram in the thicket, heard the voice from above, from within, from without:

""'STOP! Abraham! This is not the true sacrifice, and neither is the killing of a goat. No! The true sacrifice is not this cruel act of offering up the life's blood, the life breath of another, be it man or beast. No, it is the daily making sacred of each daily task, so that something rises from your world. It is the redeeming of this world by lifting it up so it may touch the higher world — that is the task for which the unique resonance and offering of each man, each woman is required."

"'That is what I heard,' said my Abraham. Then, looking at me in anguished tenderness, he told me that now Isaac, our son, my child, was to leave us for three years to complete his preparation to practise this new kind of sacrifice."

And now Sarah paused, looking at each of us slowly, and including in her gaze the entire and holy enclosure.

"Yes, my dears, he went to prepare himself as you do now, and," her voice fell to a choked whisper, "I never saw him again."

And as we turned, startled and questioning, she murmured, "My part was over you see ... and the angel of the Lord himself came for me ..."

Then she laid her old hand on mine and said, so low that I think only my cousin Elizabeth heard her, "As he himself will one day come for you ..."

Dusk was falling. My face was not visible. Its expression would have given away my terror, my puzzlement, my deep feeling for the joy, the suffering, the selflessness, the sincerity of this old woman.

Dusk was falling. Our visitors melted away, vanished. And yet, on that first evening, and all the ones that followed, I sensed their presence with us, never more so than in our silences.

But Hannah was rising up and urging us to make our way into the house before the sudden fall of night, for food had been prepared for us by the other women.

So we hastened then to wash and change into the cool, clean white robes we always wore, morning and evening, when we came together. During our meal of bread and olives, of sweet soft figs, we maintained the silence which we would all keep until the morning.

The days that followed were in no way altered. We rose before sunrise, sometimes to thick mist. We washed in the smallest possible portion of the coldest, clearest water — since it hardly ever rained we had to be aware of each precious drop. With shawls over our thin robes in the cold dawn air, we gathered among the thistles and the desert flowers on the slope to the east of the dwelling, and waited for the rising of the sun. And we prayed, praying now, this day, this now, offering our tasks, our actions, ourselves, to join with the goodness which the great light shows. We prayed that at the very least our offering would help and not hinder the world in which we live. We prayed that our acts, our intention might in some measure shift and help us to come closer to the worlds above us, to enable them to come closer, so that their fine, their subtle beneficence might penetrate our coarser world.

PART TWO - V

'For the Shekinah in the time of Abraham our father is called Sarah, and in the time of Isaac is called Rebekah ...'
(Gikatilla in *Gates of Light*)

I no longer remember if we met daily with our visitors, but it still feels as if it were so; that every afternoon — late afternoon — Hannah would signal to Elizabeth and me to lay down our work and follow her down into the olive grove.

I may not remember if we met daily, but I certainly remember each visitor as if she were here with me now.

The one after Sarah was Rebekah, the wife of Isaac, the daughter-in-law she had never met.

Now Rebekah was a beauty, strong-looking with a grave and stately beauty. She was tall too, ample, dark-haired, black-eyed, in bright robes of many reds. She wore a gold ear-ring in one ear, and her many bangles jangled when she opened her arms to us in an embracing gesture, as if she wanted to include us in every detail of her story.

"I rejoiced to hear your story," she said to Sarah. "For I too know what it is to love a son as you loved Isaac, my husband ... Ours was a very great love, yes, a very great love and immediate, Isaac's and mine. How could it have been otherwise, he dwelling by the well of living waters, and I meeting his father's faithful servant, Eleazer, surely not by chance, at the well which watered not only my father's flocks, but his family too. For the waters from both most surely flowed from the four rivers which came out of Eden itself ..."

"Tell me! Tell me!" Sarah broke in. "Tell us all the story of your first encounter!"

"I had gone down to the well towards the end of the day. I had gone with other girls to fill pitchers for my father's household. I did not often do this, since my father was the elder among the elders. But I liked to go sometimes with my friends, and also because I did not like to behave as if the task of drawing water was beneath me, for water is after all the source of life ....

"I saw a man — not young, a stranger, and ... I hesitate still to say this, but ... behind him there seemed to be a mighty shadowy figure. I thought it resembled the image I had sometimes conjured up in my mind's eye when at prayer of ... yes, I will say it, of an angel ...

"Behind the stranger there were camels, ten in all and a company of ten servants, all giving an air of courtesy and prosperity. I was filling my pitcher when the stranger asked me for a drink, which I gave him willingly. I invited him to let his men and his camels also drink from the well, which they did.

"He seemed unable to tear his eyes away from me — from my face, my every move, but not in any unbecoming or flirtatious way — more as if he was delighted with what he saw in me. It was almost as if he had been seeking me and was rejoicing at having found me. 'Whose daughter are you?' he asked at last. And when I told him I was Rebekah, the daughter of Bethuel and sister of Laban he delved into the pouch on his belt and drew out gold bracelets and a heavy gold ear-ring — and asked politely if he could adorn my ear and wrists with them.

"So amazed was I by now I let him do so, standing there obediently, the other girls looking on also struck dumb, as if we were all in a dream or a storytelling.

"'Daughter of Bethuel, might there be lodging for the night in your father's house?'

"'Indeed,' I answered. 'We most surely have room and food enough for you, your men and your camels ...'

"And then the man fell to his knees and began praying, thanking the Lord God for guiding him to me and therefore fulfilling his master, Abraham's, wishes — to find a wife for his son: Isaac, from among his own people.

"As he rose to his feet again I could not help exclaiming, 'You come from Abraham! But he is a kinsman! Everyone here knows of Abraham! Let me run ahead now and tell my mother!'

"My mother listened to my breathless tale and sent my brother, Laban, to welcome the man and his company. He led them to our tents where the camels were fed and stabled for the night.

"Water was brought so that the men could wash, and Laban invited them to sit down to a fine meal.

"'No!' said the stranger. 'I will not eat until I have explained why I am here. I am Eleazer, Abraham's servant, and I am come to seek a bride for Isaac his son, for my master wishes with all his heart that Isaac should marry a daughter from among his own kin, and when I saw your daughter at the well I knew at once that my search was over. For Isaac dwells close to the living waters and here I meet this beautiful woman also by a well which springs from that same source, the everflow of the rivers of Eden ... And then she tells me she is the daughter of Abraham's kinsman ... All day I had felt the near presence of the Shekinah herself as if she was guiding me to a bride worthy of her ...'

"My father and brother listened gravely and when Eleazer had finished speaking they bowed their heads and said, 'This is most surely the Lord God's doing. We have no right to stand in His way ... so take Rebekah and lead her to Isaac so that they may become man and wife ... but not before we have feasted together!'

"But, after the feasting and rejoicing my mother spoke with tears in her eyes and said, 'Let my child stay here with me a little longer I beg of you! She will be going far from me, so give us a little more time to be together ... a few more days is all I ask!'

"To my surprise Eleazer became quite stern and then once again I glimpsed that mighty shadowy figure at his back, turning and now revealing vast folded wings. I understood that this visit and its outcome were no ordinary affairs. I was no longer surprised at Eleazer's sternness when he said firmly, implacably but politely, 'No, I am sorry, but I cannot wait any longer. I must take her to Isaac now ... I must obey my master and the Lord God ...'

"'Well,' my brother persuaded — he was always persuasive — 'at least let Rebekah decide for herself whether to go with you now or not ...'

"And Laban beckoned me forward from where I had been seated close to my mother.

"I had felt from the moment I met Eleazer that I was under a kind of benevolent spell ... part of some great future event, so now, even though my heart was weeping at the thought of leaving my mother, I stood up and heard myself say, 'I will go with Eleazer now.'

"So my mother lovingly prepared me for the long journey, and chose the maidservants I loved most to accompany me, and, weeping once more, held me close and kissed me many times. She stood at the tent door waving to the very last, with my father and my brother close to her and comforting her.

"Then I rode out to meet the man I loved at first sight. I knew at once it was Isaac when I saw him coming towards me across the desert land, having risen up from his prayers as the camel train approached. He told me later that he too, meditating by the well of life, suddenly knew that his bride was on her way to him.

"Eleazer ran to greet this fine man and although I could not make out the words I knew the faithful servant was reporting on the success of his mission.

"Isaac interrupted Eleazer's speaking and came towards me and called me by my name. 'Rebekah', he said. Then, 'Rebekah?'

"And I said, 'Isaac? Yes, Isaac.'

"And lifted my veil.

"We looked at each other long and deeply.

"'I have waited for you,' said Isaac. 'Knowing that my beloved mother, Sarah, would guide me to a true love ... Will you come with me now to her tent which I have prepared for you, my wife, my bride?'

"'I will,' I replied.

"And as I spoke I felt the presence of the Shekinah within me, as if she had been waiting for a new form, my form, which she could inhabit, just as most surely she had once inhabited *yours*, mother Sarah.

"And I knew that from now on I was obliged to honour that presence, to try and live up to that presence within me ...

"We loved one another with a great love, Isaac and I, but even so it was many years before we had children. As if to make up for the long years of waiting, hoping, longing, I gave birth to twins.

"Esau and Jacob were never friends. They had fought long and often, and bruised my womb so much that I sometimes feared I might die from their quarrels. I consulted the priests and their wives, all wise women. 'What is happening in me?' I asked. 'Come, sit with us,' they replied, 'and let us pray to the Lord.' And for many days we worked in silence and in deep peaceful quiet, worked at prayer, to obstruct the Lord as little as possible by letting go of our concerns, our demands, until at last I heard the voice saying, 'Two kinds of people are at war in your womb, two kinds of people: the one will be concerned with the outer things of life, which are of course necessary; but the other will be born to bring to life and serve the inner world necessary for the growth of all men and women's souls ... You should know now this hard truth: you carry two babes in your womb. The one who will be born first is the form of man's lower nature, earthy, fleshly, concerned with the ordinary life; the last born is the form of man's higher nature, inclined to love the seeking of, the opening to, the upper world. Both natures are necessary to bring about the clash of opposites which alone can produce a new way of being, so that men and women can hear the voice and answer as Abraham did: 'Here am I!'

"Then the priest said something utterly mysterious which," — and here Rebekah paused and again her gaze fell for some time upon me, "which, I confess, I only understood when I was invited to come here and told why I was invited. The priest said in a low voice, almost as if he was talking to himself, 'We have now two sons in the womb of Rebekah. But there will come a day when the two natures will no longer be at war with one another, but be <u>reconciled in one form</u>, and form and emptiness will meet and dwell together ...'

"Of course I did not understand the meaning of these words, but I did understand that I had no choice but to carry these quarrelling babes and bring them forth.

"Filled with awe I bowed my head and said, 'So be it. My soul magnifies the Lord, for he hath regarded the lowliness of his handmaiden, for behold from henceforth all generations shall call me blessed ...'

And Rebekah looked at me, Maryam, with a tender smile and said, "These words will rise up in *you* one day, dear child ..." and I trembled but did not know why I trembled.

Then Rebekah returned to her story.

"Before I left we all prayed for help for me. Red-haired Esau the larger, more robust baby came forth first with a healthy howl, and little, dark-haired Jacob came out clutching his brother's heel, as if till the very last he had been trying to push past his brother and become the natural first-born. It was Jacob who was first on his feet; Jacob who was the first to speak. I could not help myself ... my heart inclined towards this beguiling and precocious son just as Isaac's was touched by rugged Esau, who from an early age proved to be a fighter, a hunter, a man of the fields.

"One day, Esau came in hungry from the fields and begged his brother, implored his brother to let him eat his fill of the lentils Jacob had prepared for himself. 'Very well,' Jacob at last agreed, 'but on one condition ...'

"'What condition? Any condition you ask!'

"'I want your birthright.'

'Birthright! Birthright! Words, just words! Have it! Have it! Pass me the bowl! I am famished, starved, dying of hunger ...!'

"It was when I learnt what had taken place that I became certain that something special was going to be demanded of Jacob. I vowed to help him in every way I could. I say 'I vowed' but I have long since come to believe that it was not 'I' but the voice of the Shekinah dwelling within me, commanding me ... this voice which sounds both from within and without and has nothing to do with the small concerns of any one of us.

"Suddenly I understood that the blessing-prayer my parents bestowed on me when I married Isaac, and which had for so long seemed to have been to no avail — that I would be the source of the seed of many, was perhaps to be fulfilled through this child of mine, Jacob.

"I saw that Jacob would need his father's blessing before he could proceed on his destined path.

"I knew that Isaac in fact preferred Esau to Jacob. This puzzled me — that my serious, inwardly turned, pious husband should be so drawn to the rough and ready ways of Esau seemed incomprehensible. I also realised that this very preference would only add to my attempts to help Jacob achieve I knew not what.

"I brooded over this much and often, but it was not until the boys were thirteen that I returned to the court, the academy of priests.

"'Ah,' breathed the old rabbi when I put my question to him. I immediately felt relieved and sat back and listened to the deep, questioning silence that filled the simple room, where the other priests — and their wise wives — sat against the whitewashed walls.

"'Ah ...,' the old man breathed. 'Indeed at first sight it does seem incomprehensible, but let us go deeper into the matter. Already in the womb there was a struggle between the two babes — Esau the lower nature fighting with Jacob, the higher nature. They could be said to be the two sides of the one man ... Why did Jacob pull down on Esau's heel; you told us he came out clinging to it? He knew that the life force, the primeval "serpent" was now in the form of his brother, and that he would have to pull him down to prevent him from gaining the upper hand ... prevent the lower nature from defiling the Sanctuary, from overwhelming and putting to sleep the other. I believe that when Jacob was born YHVH said "Behold! here is one who can stand up to the serpent force." He will have cunning — you will see — Jacob will deal with Esau slyly, through cunning ... he will always have to have his wits about him to prevent Esau's nature from prevailing over his.

"'Now, as to why Isaac prefers Esau to Jacob ...

"'Isaac your husband is no ordinary man. In future times he will be seen to be — with his father, Abraham and his son, Jacob, one part of the triadic pillar of the world below — which mirrors the world above. Indeed Isaac is no ordinary man, for who else has ever been bound and prepared for sacrifice by his own father and accepted it? Yes, his attribute is rigour, but by his acceptance of his binding for sacrifice he was rewarded with the power to blend his rigour with mercy. Therefore he has taken upon himself to draw Esau away in order to make it possible for what is intended for Jacob to take place ... I tell you these things, Rebekah, to help you to keep the space in you open to the Shekinah, that she may dwell in you as the intentions of the Lord unfold. You have a role to play there — not <u>you</u> but that divine presence in you. How can I convince you, Rebekah, that your story is already written? The ram, for instance — the ram, which Isaac must surely have told you, suddenly seemed to appear in the thicket and took his place for the sacrifice, this ram was no ordinary ram either. This ram had been created by the Lord in the twilight of the first Sabbath and kept waiting for this moment. This ram was running towards Abraham and Isaac when the devil tried to stop it by entangling it in the thicket ... And I should tell you also that when the sacrifice was accomplished Abraham took the most tender care of the ram's remains. In gratitude to this creature he and Isaac gathered up its ashes which later formed the inner altar of Solomon's Temple. King David himself inherited the sinews of the ram from which he made ten of the strings of his harp; Elijah's girdle was fashioned out of its skin. As for its horns — one was blown on Mount Sinai by Moses himself, at the end of the reading out of the Ten Commandments; the other waits for the day when all our people will come together to that Mount Moriah where the sacrifice took place. All will return there from the cruel exiles which await our people — and by that time a great city will have grown up there — the city of Yerushalayim. No participant in this story is ordinary, none there by chance. It is all foreseen ...

"'Your husband Isaac has a suffering, painful part to play. How would we know about light if it were not for darkness? Isaac's attribute is a dark one. You have remarked on how quiet he is, how serious, how inwardly turned, and he was so from that day on the mountain; he was so when he came towards you in the desert and you loved him for it. He is the pure sacrifice, and who, therefore, is to say that the way he is with Esau is not part of that sacrifice? It would take a far wiser man than I am to explain fully why Isaac acts as he does now with Esau. If you feel that Isaac risks to besmirch his soul because of this other kind of sacrifice, I can tell you that he said to me the last time I went to sit with him, "How I continue to praise the Lord because he has given us degrees of souls — I am not afraid. I ask Esau to hunt for me and bring me his game. I know that sometimes he is too lazy even to do that and brings me foul meat from some stray beast, but the 'blessings' we exchange do not touch more than my most lowly soul which takes upon itself to protect the others ..."

"'Oh yes, dear Rebekah, your husband may now be old and his eyes are dim. He is almost blind. Could this poor sight come only from the years of living in the smoky tents of Esau's wives, who are always burning oil lamps of worship to their own gods? Or does it come from the tears which the angels shed as they watched him bare his neck to his father's knife? Or is it because he deliberately does not look closely at the acts of Esau? He knows why he acts as he does. How could it be otherwise?

"'You must trust, dear Rebekah, you must trust that this story is not yours, ours, but the Lord's and the more you trust, the more space there will be for the Shekinah to dwell within you. She will no longer come passing by for a minute here, a minute there, but enter into you for good ... and then the deeds you have to undertake and the seeming deceptions on the part of you and of Isaac, will have the blessing of the Lord ...'

"He paused as if waiting for me to absorb all he had said. Then with a gentle smile he said, 'Before you return to your tents shall we all pray together?'

"And I do not know if it was because it was not my usual solitary attempt at prayer but the combined prayers of all of those present, I tasted trust during the moments which followed. Yes, trust, in the teeth of the peril which is true prayer, because it demands the risk of putting all into the hands of some higher force than mine. A trust which left me vulnerable, but also open ...

"And so I returned home, my days never to be the same again. The openness remained and grew. It was like a strange pregnancy — of emptying, not of filling. The emptier I seemed the more I sensed. There was my beating heart, my breathing, my blood circulation. There were the tears that sometimes fell from my eyes for no apparent reason. There was the straightening and strengthening of my spine, but not into a stiffness, but into the flexibility of a reed giving way to the force of the invisible wind. I knew then that the Shekinah had come into me and that it was she who was guiding me.

"Not long after my visit to the priest, I heard Isaac call out to Esau and say: 'I am old. My days are coming to an end. I have a father's blessing to give to you, my first-born. Therefore go out into the fields and bring me venison and fetch good wine, that we may celebrate together when the blessing is over.'

"My heart lurched but I calmed it.

"I went with quiet steps to Jacob and said to him firmly: 'Jacob my son, listen to me, and do everything that I will tell you to do.'

"He looked at me closely.

"'I see a special light in your eyes, mother. Your voice is scarcely your own. Therefore I will ask no questions but obey you in everything ...'

"'Go out into the fields and kill and skin two kids and bring them to me that I may prepare a delicious dish for your father. For this is the day on which he will give you the blessing a father always gives his son when he feels that he is nearing the end of his life ...'

"Jacob turned away and I knew he was weeping.

"'No, Jacob. Do not weep,' I heard myself (if it was I) say. 'Go and do as I say and all will be well ...'

"Away he went and when he returned with the two skinned kids and the stew was simmering on the stove, I said to him, 'And now go and fetch the sacred garments which have come down to Esau from your grandfather, Abraham, and which I keep in my wedding chest ...'

"He did so and I put them on him, these special garments with a sweet scent and I sewed the skins of the kids onto his arms and sent him into his father.

"Then I concealed myself in the curtains of the doorway to Isaac's tent.

"As I stood there I felt filled with the presence, and knew that all that was taking place was wished for by the Whole on High.

"I heard Isaac ask: 'Who is there?'

"And Jacob's response: 'It is I, father, Esau, thy first-born.'

"I could tell that Isaac was uncertain of this answer and I trembled when I heard him say, 'Come closer, my son, so I may touch you ...'

"Jacob obeyed and Isaac groped first at his garments and then found his arms.

"'The arms, the hands are Esau's, but the voice is Jacob's ...' I heard him murmur, and then hesitate — as if listening to an inner voice, and at the same time I heard the one within me say. *Bless Jacob — though his descendants will vex the Lord, and be scattered in exile across the face of the earth; though he and they are fallible they know there is a Lord to love, a mystery to behold with awe, an aim in view, a journey to made* ... and then I heard Isaac say, 'The voice of Jacob shall prevail, because it is intended to praise the Whole on High. Come closer, my son, that I may bless you with a father's blessing ...'

"As this was taking place, Jacob drew closer and closer to his father, who suddenly smiled as if he had been freed of a heavy burden.

"'Ah,' he said, 'I smell the sweetness upon you, the sweetness of those holy garments which came down to us from my beloved father, Abraham, and I know now that indeed you should receive my blessing ...'

"Jacob sank to his knees in front of his father.

"I was near to tears, but she who dwelt within me, she rejoiced because she knew now that the great story would continue to unfold.

"As Jacob stood up again I saw that he was transformed. There was a new beauty on him, as if the blessing had penetrated to his very marrow. For although it was Isaac who had pronounced the blessing we all knew its true source.

"And then, suddenly — as I was gazing on the joyful, fulfilled expression on Jacob's face; as Isaac was sitting back quietly, we all heard Esau's noisy arrival.

"Jacob just had time to slip away before his brother saw him.

"I drew back deeper among the tent's dark folds, but I was still able to hear what took place between Esau and his father.

"'Get up, father,' I heard Esau say roughly, and the sound of a dish being slammed down ...

"'Get up! Come on! Come and eat this meat I have prepared for you. I have had enough trouble getting it so hurry up and eat it ...'

"'I must tell you, my son, that your brother has already prepared meats for me which I have eaten ...'

"'Meats!' cried Esa, 'Meats! And to think I sold him my birthright for a humble bowl of lentils!'

"'You sold Jacob your birthright?'

"'Yes, father ... I was hungry ... famished ... At the time it did not seem so important ...'

"'Not important? Sold to assuage your bodily hunger? The birthright which would have entitled you to oversee the sacred acts of the family's daily life? The birthright which would have made you almost a priest?'

"'Huh! I never did much care for those matters ... you know that, father! You know I love a more robust way of life! Hunting, drinking, seeking out beautiful women to make my own ... the pleasures of this world. I don't much believe in any other!'

"I heard Isaac groan and then after a long silence I heard him say, 'Now I know. Now I know and can die in peace, for I am sure I gave my blessing rightly to your brother, Jacob ...'

"At this Esau let out a howl of pain.

"'You have given Jacob the blessing which rightfully belongs to me! How could you father? How could you?'

"And he began to weep loudly.

"'No, my son, it was not I who gave the blessing, but the Whole on High. I sensed the presence of the Shekinah herself. I was just the vessel, the instrument ... And besides now I learn that you had already sold your birthright for a bowl of soup, I know that the blessing has gone to the right man. Nevertheless, my heart aches for you and so I will bless you with my own blessing, that you may enjoy all the riches and pleasures of this world until your dying day ...'

"Isaac put out his hands here towards Esau and would indeed have blessed him kindly, but Esau stepped out of his reach, crying, 'If I lay my hands on ... when I lay my hands on Jacob I will most surely kill him ...'

"And he turned on his heel, ran out into the blinding mid-day sun in a blind rage and went this way and that in fruitless search of his brother.

"On that day, at that hour, it seemed utterly impossible to believe that a day would come, a day far, far in the future when these brothers, these twins, would meet on a dusty road and in some degree, be reconciled ..."

PART TWO - VI

"And this is why ..."

"Jacob came to us ..."

"To me ..."

"To us ..."

Two voices like the cooing of turtle doves interrupted Rebekah.

Leah and Rachel, side by side and speaking in turn, but without rancour, Rachel, if anything, deferring to her sister.

They too, like Esau and Jacob, were twins, but who lived in harmony with each other, finishing each other's sentences, sitting close to one another, hands touching ... frequently looking at the other as if to confirm, to concur ...

Rebekah smiled at them.

"Yes, indeed," she agreed. "That was when and why I sent him to you — or, rather to your father, my brother Laban. I feared that Esau would not rest until he had found and killed his brother so, while Esau was running hither and thither in his blind rage, I sought out Jacob where I knew I would find him — at work among the shepherds with Esau's own sheep — the last place his brother would think of ..."

"And it was on his way to ..."

"Me ..."

"Us ..."

"He had the vision ..."

"in the solitary place ..."

"in the dark night ..."

"the vision of the ladder reaching between heaven and earth with all the angels coming and going ..."

"ascending ..."

"and descending ..."

They spoke in turn, but in accord, affectionately, amiably.

"And then he came to the well ..."

"That same well," Rebekah interrupted, "where I met Eleazer, Abraham's servant in search of a bride for Isaac, Jacob's father."

"And I was there," said Rachel.

"In all your beauty," said Leah, "And he fell in love with you ..."

"But he married *you* first, for it was your destiny to give birth to six of his twelve sons ... while I ... I was destined to give birth to only two of them — my beautiful Joseph and my little Benjamin, the last of the line ..."

"And some say those two were the first Tzaddikim, the first Righteous Men. For without Joseph the children of Israel would not have been saved from death by starvation; would not have survived to multiply and spread as the waters cover the sea ..."

"Poor Jacob," sighed Rachel with a tender smile.

"Yes - he did not understand — not at first ..."

"Not until much later ..."

"He did not understand ..."

"What we understood from the beginning ..."

"In his impatience for *you*, Rachel ..."

"And his anger at our crafty father ..."

"He forgot to study the meaning of our names ..."

"He forgot to study their letters — **"lamed aleph hey, Leah** ... the **lamed** at the beginning of my name would have shown I was connected to above and below ..."

"and the **lamed** at the end of my name, Rachel, **resh, heth, lamed**, would have shown him that I had further to go to attain that connection ..."

"He did not understand then that only through the two of us would he become unceasingly joined to the life on high and the life on this earth ..."

"Nor did he understand that the two of us were needed to complete the sturdy pillars of the four mothers ..."

"The other two, of course, being you, Sarah, and you, Rebekah ..."

"Four pillars, four mothers ..."

"Four virtuous women *whose price is far above rubies* ..."

"Whose husbands can trust in them ..."

"*Who are not afraid of the snow for their households ...*"

"*For they are all clothed in wool from their looms ...*"

"Four virtuous women, *whose clothing is strength and wisdom ...* "

"Four virtuous women, *whose husbands are known in the gates, where they sit among the elders of the land ...*"

"Four virtuous women who live in awe of the Lord ..."

"Who sustain and hold up the canopy of the sacred ..."

"Who prepare the Sabbath ..."

"Light the candles ..."

"Bake the bread ..."

"Fetch the wine in the pitchers ..."

"Who make the place and the space for the presence to fill ..."

"We are the action itself which makes possible the contemplation ..."

They paused, and Rebekah turned to me, Maryam, and said, "Now do you see the pattern, dear one? Now do you see all the rich preparation, the lives and the living that have gone before — and of which you are becoming a part as the stories seep into you and you begin to understand that there is only the one consciousness, only one intention — to help the Whole on High to descend ... ?"

I bowed my head and murmured, "Indeed I do see and I am grateful ... I feared that something was expected of me from out of nothing, from out of my own ignorance and nothingness ... and now I know that there is this great past to lean against like the solid trunk of a great tree, from which I will be able to take strength for this task, which is only beginning to outline its shape and even less so its full meaning ..."

I think Rebekah wanted to respond to me but *the voices of the turtle doves* were once more *heard in the land*, but now more as if they were talking only to each other, forgetting for the moment that they were not alone ...

"Of course, Jacob despised me," Leah was saying sadly rather than bitterly. "That was hurtful ..."

"But you were consoled," Rachel insisted.

"A little ..."

"By knowing the true reasons, the true intention ..."

"Yes, but it is easy to forget high matters when day by day, year by year I had to ask him to give me his children, beg him, trick him ... and hear him breathe your name as I lay there conceiving his children ..."

"We both paid heavy prices ... at least you gave him six sons ..."

"And a daughter ..."

"And I only two ..."

"But," said Leah, generous not only in her body but in her heart, "but it was to you that Jacob described the encounter ..."

"It was surely not mere chance that he experienced it as we were returning, all of us, to his real homeland ..."

"Indeed not — and remember! He saw the ladder on his way to us ..."

"He *dreamt* he saw ..."

"He dreamt he saw the ladder and the angels ..."

"And saw the Lord and heard the voice saying, I AM with you ..."

"His first experience of awe ..."

"As he set out on a journey into the unknown ..."

"And the second?"

"A dream?"

"A vision?"

"A visitation, I call it ... A visitation at dawn ..."

"A being ..."

"An angel?"

"The angel of the Lord?"

"The Lord himself?"

"Jacob challenged him at once ..."

"And wrestled with him, struggled for his life ..."

"With a great being ..."

"Who could not bring him down ..."

"Until he pulled on Jacob's thigh ..."

"But even then, Jacob would not let him go ..."

"Until he'd blessed him and been given a new name ..."

"Israel," the sisters finished in chorus.

"And with this new name, a new beginning ..."

"And he gathered together all his twelve sons ..."

"Reuben, Simeon and Levi ..."

"Judah, Issachar and Zebulon ... my six sons," said Leah, not without pride.

"Dan, Naphtali — the sons of my handmaid, Billhah", added Rachel with a sigh, "and then my own, my Joseph, and on the long journey home with much travail, the little Benjamin for whom I gave up my life ..."

"Lastly," said Leah, "there were Gad and Asher, the sons of *my* maidservant, Zilpah ..."

"The first children of Israel," said Rachel.

"Making certain that the story could continue ..."

"Sarah! Rebekah! Leah! Rachel!" came the voice of my mother, Hannah, into the vibrant silence which fell when the sisters' dovelike voices finally ceased. "We salute you, the first mothers, the four who with their devotion to their husbands and their love of their sons, enabled the story to unfold. You sanctified the Sabbath by seeing that the breads were baked, the wines pressed, the lamps trimmed, the oil jars filled, the tents swept; the rugs beaten, the bowls for washing of hands filled with fresh cool water; you, by attending to the forms made it possible for the formless to enter with blessings and love and wisdom and guidance ... We salute you! We honour you! And ask you now to encourage the great-grandmother of King David to tell her story."

PART TWO - VII

'The Lord do so to me, and more also, if aught but death part thee and me ... '

Hannah, my mother, turned to Ruth, little brown bird, shy, self-effacing ...

She did not speak immediately, but seemed to be gathering up her courage first of all to raise her downcast eyes, look round at us all, then rest her gaze on me ...

"I do not know what worth there is for you, dear Maryam, in my short tale ...

"Born a Moabite, raised to worship other gods, but I can sing the praises of my Hebrew mother-in-law, Naomi, without whom I would not have played the part I did in the bringing into existence the ancestors of David the beloved, David the psalmist, David the fallible king, David, the father of Solomon himself ...

"If I was a Moabite how, you will ask, did I come to be married to a Hebrew? My husband, Chilion, was the son of Elimelech. A rich, highly influential man in his own country, when famine struck that land, instead of helping the starving, Elimelech fled with his wife and two sons into the land of Moab. There, he soon attracted my father's attention because of his wealth and his aristocratic bearing. Before long my father made him part of his powerful inner circle, and, in time also made my husband and his brother generals in his army. Elimelech and his sons were flattered. They enjoyed their importance, their wealth, the worldly life of my father's court.

"I had no say in my marriage. It was my father's wish or, you could say, his command. My sister, Orpah, had been given in marriage to my husband's brother, Mahlon. She and I could not have been more different. She loved the life of an army wife — the freedom it gave her when Mahlon was away, the feasting and dancing at our father's palace when the army returned to the city ...

"But I endured this life with great difficulty, and waited with secret longing for the times when the men were away skirmishing on our frontiers, or on long falcon hunts in the desert hinterland.

"Then I would creep away to Naomi, our mother-in-law.

"I had never met a woman like her. Modest, not given to idle chatter, diligent, kind to her servants, she kept a good house. The floors were always swept, the rugs beaten, the copper bowls shining, her linen as white as the snow on the peaks of Mount Tabor. I noticed that she took immense care with her cooking. Her delicious goat's cheese and milk, for example, were always served separately from the goat's meat. Her bread unleavened. Once a week — and every week — at the moment when the first star appeared she would light candles and prepare a table with fresh bread made with egg, and fill goblets with good wine ... And then she would sit and wait and let me know without a word that perhaps it was time for me to go. I understood later that she was waiting for her men to come home for Sabbath. And I think it was observing these rituals which made me wonder — where were *her* gods?

"Eventually I found the courage to ask her, 'Where is your altar, Naomi? What gods do you worship?'

"'My altar is within,' she replied.

"It was as if she were speaking a foreign language — and one, I found, I suddenly desperately wanted to learn.

"'I do not need any other altar. My God is one and invisible. My God is both above me and within me. His commandments dwell in my heart. My task is to try to make whole and sacred each daily moment, each breath, each step, each task. My task is to praise and give thanks for the world I live in. My task is to touch the lintel of my door at my going out and my coming in to remind me of my task.'

"'One? Invisible? No little clay idols to align on a flat stone; little clay idols to fear, and to placate with offerings of all kinds?'

"'Fear, not,' said Naomi. 'Awe, yes; awe which grows into love. Love of the One and only of the One ... the love made manifest by obedience to the commandments Moses brought back down from Mount Sinai. There are to be no graven images of the One; no misuse or abuse of that name. The seventh day of each week is to be kept holy and devoted to the One, leaving aside all other work. We must honour the father and the mother, the ancestors back to our first parents, Adam and Eva. There is to be no murder — neither of another human being nor in thought and feeling; no adultery — neither with another's spouse, nor by stirring holiness with the profane in an unholy cauldron; no lies about one's neighbour, no use of malice or unkindness, which might slander him or her, not even by silly gossip; no to desiring one's neighbour's wife or husband; no coveting of that neighbour's possessions, however poor one might seem in comparison ... '

"As the years went by I found the courage to ask her questions, many questions about her God, her faith, which she always answered as if it were a real joy for her to share her innermost world with me. It grew to be a joy for me also, because slowly but surely I began to feel that I had found something I hardly knew I had been searching for — a deeper, higher vision of what it might mean to feel that I had a place, a role to play. Naomi's understanding of a god, of God, assumed a relationship — intimate, active, serving a purpose, between this high force emanating its great rays down upon us. It was a very different experience from the way we Moabites worshipped.

"And then Elimelech died and slowly but inexorably the family's fortunes changed; my father lost interest in them; my husband and his brother began to drink and gamble. We lost all our money and then one after the other the brothers fell mortally ill.

"A day came when Naomi said, tears streaming down her face: 'I have lived long enough in this alien land. And now my only wish is to go home. Do not try to dissuade me, dear daughters. Moab is your country; you will most surely find new husbands among your own people. I thank you both for loving my sons, but they are gone and there is nothing to keep me here one day more ... Walk with me, if you wish, the last few miles to the border and there let us say our farewells ... '

"We did not try to dissuade her — Orpah had never cared much for Naomi anyway, and I knew it was useless to try and persuade her to change her mind.

"So we set off along the white dusty path, three women in mourning clothes.

"My heart grew heavier at every step. I could not bear the thought of being parted from this woman I had come to love as a mother. In her I had found a spirituality. I could not bear it that we would never again talk together of her God, her faith; never again watch her plait the Sabbath bread or bring the candlesticks to a brighter shine.

"'Well, my dears,' Naomi said when we reached the border, 'let me embrace you both one more time and then you must leave me and go home … '

"Orpah kissed her lightly, almost gaily, as if Naomi's departure was a signal that now she was as free as air. She set off immediately, turning just once with a little wave.

"'But I fell on Naomi's neck and clung to her, kissing her and weeping.

"She tried to comfort me, but it was no good and then, suddenly and at once I knew I was not going to go home. I was going to go with her, so I stepped back and said, 'No, Naomi. I cannot say good-bye. I cannot return home. My home is with you now, and I am coming with you … No, don't try to stop me … Where you are going I am going too … '

"'Dear child,' she said, 'you don't know what you are saying! The laws of my land are strict — you will not be welcome — a pagan Moabite. No man will want to marry you … '

"'But I don't want to stay a pagan Moabite!' I cried. 'I want your God to be my God; I want your people to be my people, and when the time comes for me to die I want to be buried next to you. From this day on, nothing but death can part me from you! Surely you must know by now what you mean to me — you and your faith? All these years I have watched you, asked you questions, pondered on your answers; all these years my love and respect for you has grown and deepened. But perhaps it is only now at this moment that I really understand how much you mean to me! You cannot turn me away now! I will surely wither and die … !'

"'Ruth! Ruth!' said Naomi, taking me in her arms again. 'Oh, Ruth! What shall I do with you! Well, come with me, child, daughter. Come with me and together we will try to make a place for ourselves in the Hebrew world.'

"It was as Naomi had feared. She was welcomed coolly by her kinsmen — who remembered how her husband had left them all to survive a famine or not. It did not help her having me at her side. None of them offered her a place to stay; we had to find a small room in the poorer part of the city of Bethlehem, where we lived very quietly and with very little food. We were so poor, so hungry that I would go out into the fields to glean the fallen stalks of barley — as the law allowed.

"But all that changed once Boaz had visited her. Boaz was also a kinsman — a distant one, a wealthy one but above all a kind one. He too had recently been widowed, and I felt his sympathy for this cousin, no longer young, and without a husband.

"As for me, I felt accepted courteously, unquestioningly, and this before Naomi explained to him who I was, and that I wished to enter school and study the Torah as soon as possible in order to embrace fully my new found ever more beloved faith.

"He at once offered us a little house for which he refused any rent.

"And when Naomi wept and tried to thank him, he brushed off the generosity by saying, 'It is nothing, Naomi, and you know it. Surely you have not forgotten the obligations of blood by which our people abide. Moreover, I have seen Ruth amid the corn and how she never takes more than is her due. And I would like to offer her now to come to my fields where she may pick up all that falls and share the mid-day meal. This will relieve a little your need until you have had time to sell the land which once belonged to your husband ... '

"And so each day I would go to the fields belonging to Boaz. I became aware only slowly that he was almost always there, and how his gaze would rest on me at the meal-time, but gently and never for longer than was acceptable. Sometimes he would bring figs for us wrapped in vine leaves, or a cluster of grapes which I would carry home carefully so as not to bruise the sweet ripe fruits.

"Now comes my confession. I have listened to the tales of all the other women here and heard that nothing was achieved without the use of cunning — only in order that the Lord God's will should be accomplished. But it may surprise you when I tell you that it was Naomi's idea that I should encourage Boaz to take me as his wife.

"'Indeed,' she told me, 'as a kinsman of both our husbands, he is entitled to marry you according to our laws. It is clear that he finds you desirable, but perhaps he hesitates to ask you because he is so much older than you ...

"'Now, listen to me. You know that Boaz sleeps every night on the threshing floor – not only to guard his grain, but also because he rises as early as his labourers and often works with them in the fields. I want you to put on your old bridal dress and what bridal jewels you have left ("she knew, you see, that I had been selling my jewels to pay for our daily needs"). You may cover yourself with your old brown cloak. Then go down to him at nightfall and lie down at his feet ... '

"'But, mother!' I protested. 'I am not a brazen woman!'

"'I know that,' said Naomi, 'and so does Boaz. He will not take advantage of you, but he will understand what he must do and he will do it. You will make him happy; he is a good man; he knows we are destitute; he will look after you and you will look after me. And, who knows, you may not die childless.'

"Naomi knew how much I wished I had a child. I could see that my act would bring happiness and peace of mind to all of us, so ... I agreed. As night fell I walked down to the threshing barns and quietly lay down beside Boaz. I think he was at first astonished to find me there, but all came to pass as Naomi had said it would. He kissed my hands and said, 'Ruth, little dove! I should have asked you long ago and not left it to you to seek me out. I dearly wish to ask you to be my wife, but although I have this right, there is, sad to say, another kinsman who is even more closely related to your husband than I am, and first I am obliged to ask him if he wishes to buy Naomi's fields and marry you. So now, get up and go home before the sun rises. I would not wish you to be seen here by everyone else.'

"And when I rose to go, he hastily filled a small sack with barley and thrust it into my arms. 'This way they will just think you came early for grain for today's bread. Now go home and I will seek out this kinsman as soon as the sun is up.'

"The wishes of the Lord must have been with us all that day for it turned out that this other man was not prepared to marry a foreign woman and a Moabitess at that. He gave up his rights then and there to redeem the fields and me. So again Naomi was right. We were married a few days later. I gave birth to a son, Obed, who was the joy of his father's old age and the light of my eye. And I rejoiced each time I saw Naomi holding him in her arms. Obed was the father of Jesse, who in turn was the father of King David, the beloved, no less ... and I was blessed even more because not only did I live to see the day that David brought the Ark of the Covenant into the Temple in Jerusalem, but I was there to witness the birth of Solomon himself ..."

She paused and looked at us all, still blushing slightly from her confession, but with a certain tilt of pride to her chin.

"If Elimelech had not gone to Moab; if I had not married his son; if Naomi had not been devout; if she had succeeded in sending me away; if Boaz had not married me and Obed had not been born, there would have been no Jesse, and no father to care for the child that Maryam will bear ..."

With Ruth's eye upon me, I felt as if I had been struck by lightning, sitting there on that warm dry earth ... I wanted to speak, to ask, but she was still speaking determinedly.

"All we women, it seems," she then said, "through certain deceits and slyness, helped to bring about great events ... It has ever been so ... until now, sweet Maryam ..."

And she was looking at me alone now. "Until now, sweet Maryam. With you there will be no guile, no cunning — or will there? I see far ahead of you the moment when you will have the courage or the cunning to help bring about your son's first miracle making."

I gasped. I tried to speak, to ask what? What are you telling me? What are you all telling me?

A tear, then another, and another trickled down my cheek. Hannah, my mother, saw and sent a radiant and reassuring smile down the *mandorla* to lighten my heart and dry my tears.

"Let us stop now, sisters," she said firmly. "Come, my child, come, Elizabeth, let us go and help with the evening work, and then we will deserve some of those same sweet fruits which Boaz once brought to Ruth and Naomi."

And as we walked slowly out of the olive grove, she murmured softly, "Patience, patience, daughter. The *mandorla* is nearly complete ..."

As I have said before, I think, I do not remember now exactly how our visitors left us at the end of our meetings. They just seemed to fade and vanish, leaving my mother, Elizabeth and myself to return to the others in the house of preparation, as if we had been alone, perhaps studying in the olive grove. Nor do I remember whether the visitors spoke one after the other or if there were gaps of days between each encounter.

But I do remember that evening when my mother saw my tears and assured me that the *mandorla* was nearly complete.

Jenny Koralek

PART TWO – VIII

'And in all the land there were no women found so fair as the daughters of Job, and their father gave them inheritance among their brethren.'

And I *do* remember the afternoon when the three daughters of Job appeared in the olive grove and sank down beside Rachel and Ruth.

They were exceedingly beautiful. Even though their simple rose-madder dresses were so plain that it seemed that they might just have taken off aprons, and just smoothed their rich dark hair after milking their goats, or kneading their dough and leaving it to rise in order to join us.

And indeed I am glad — have always been glad — that I had not fled and hidden after my weeping and bewilderment when Ruth had finished her story.

Glad because of all the women I had listened to, I later came to understand that it was these three sisters, these daughters of Job who had had most to teach me of the only way I would be able to withstand what I would have to go through.

Jemima, Kezia, Kerenheppuch, were, like Job, their father, ordinary, hardworking, very much engaged in the material acts of daily life in this earthly world, but all pervaded by a deep trust in the Whole on High, all always trying to offer all their acts, however small, however great, to that Whole on High.

Daughters of Job, whose name contains the immense meaning that he was at each moment in touch with all the emanations coming down from on high, that he was the dwelling-place for this help ...

Daughters of Job, whose inheritance '*among their brethren*' was not only land and sheep, goats and camels, but their father's understanding of the need for a faithful and persistent search for a direct experience of God, of YHVH, of I AM ... to accept to be pierced by it, permeated by it, afflicted by it.

Job had had a doubting thought. He was suddenly dissatisfied with his piety, seeing it consisted only of outward forms.

Devout to a fault, from dawn to dusk, impeccable in obedience to all the laws, never forgetting the prayers, the blessings, his doubt was – did he really know 'God'?

"Many evenings we sat with him in the cooling air," Jemima began, "just before the sun's last swift sinking, the scent of the day breathing into us, thyme and lavender, and the bread baked and the lamb roasted; the last bleat of lambs and kids before darkness; the murmurs of women in the kitchen; the number of men's voices above the splash of water in the stream as they washed their feet and hands, dabbed away at sweaty faces and beards before supper, after the long day in the sun, the pastures, the olive groves ...

"'I was visited by doubt.'

"That is what he told us," said Jemima. 'As if I was being tested,' he said ...

"'I do not know if the doubt was mine or His,' he said."

"Who knows?" put in Kezia, "who knows — was it God who doubted our father and decided to put him to the test ... ?"

"Or was it the great adversary himself? Was it Satan, demanding to be allowed to test him to the limits?" added Kerenheppuch. "It started when all our father's livestock, his asses, his oxen, his camels were stolen away, his shepherds and ploughman murdered by marauding bands, his sheep struck by a savage storm of lightning and hail stones the size of herons' eggs ... And then, oh grief of griefs, his first family, his sons and daughters were all killed when a great tempest brought the house down upon them ..."

"Wounded," said Kezia, "indeed, broken-hearted, he rent his garments, yet somehow he still kept his faith and was able to bow his head and acknowledge that the Lord had given, the Lord had taken away, but he was still able to bless the name of the Lord ..."

"'My relation to the Lord remained unchanged,' he told us," said Jemima. "'My relation to the Lord remained unchanged until ...

"'until I was afflicted, wounded in the flesh, in my own flesh, and knew pain, unremitting pain, and found my pious prayers and salutations, my ritual washings and fastings and sayings of grace before meals healed me not by one cell. You see, I thought I knew the Lord; that my faithful forms of worship, my devout daily conduct was sufficient, would please him, propitiate him; that it was enough to be an unthinking faithful servant; that he would take care of the rest, take care of me. Yes, I thought I had already met the Lord through the forms of my acts. It was of course too easy, too smooth running, until my body was covered in sores which wept and itched and never seemed to heal — or if they did in one place, they would break out in another.

"'But it was not the physical fleshly sores in themselves ... it was the experience of being assailed directly, challenged, confronted ...

"'"Curse God," said your mother. "Curse God and die ..." I called her foolish, and told her to hold her tongue and yet, perhaps she was not foolish, but voicing that longing in all of us to make an end of what is intolerable, seek someone to blame and then to give up. I should have been grateful that she said this, because in my state, clouded by pain and intense irritation and desperation it was like the slap administered to an hysteric. I came to myself and decided No, I would not curse God, I would not die, I would sit there and endure, finally acknowledge my deep lack of understanding, that I did not know God at all, that I must stay there with my suffering, stay there with my questions, stay there doggedly, knowing I would waver very often, very often indeed, that I would try to escape, seek answers, explanations; that to admit I did not know God <u>at all</u> was necessary in order to grow in understanding; that I had to give up all that had been and face that not knowing.'

"'It was torment,' he told us," said Jemima. "'It was hell. Never more so than when well-meaning friends decided to join me, sit with me, and hold forth to me for what seemed eternity on the fact of my sinfulness. They were convinced beyond the shadow of a doubt that it was this which had angered God and this was my punishment from him ... Strangely enough, the more they blamed me, the more convinced I was that this was not so. Yes, of course, I was a sinner, but that was not why God had punished me. God had not punished me, I began to see. It was nothing to do with God. Unfortunate and terrible events, followed by disease, to which all men are prey, had come of themselves and all the doubt was mine, the punishing was mine. And so I began to reflect.

"'Study your name,' said an inner voice. 'The name to which you were given. It is telling you there is a link for you with the Whole on High. You have the possibility to understand; you must live each moment, neither looking to the past, nor toward the future, but filling the present with your presence. The suffering of your body could annihilate you, but it could also oblige you to bear it for a time. You cannot escape — this is a direct experience of a true encounter with that Whole on High ... '

"'And so I sat and sat and sat, not knowing what would come of this, listening to the well-meaning comforters, putting my own arguments until we all had headaches ... and all the time I knew that here were no answers, no explanations, and then suddenly one day, I cried out that I knew God existed. Whatever else, I knew that He did exist and that in some way I did not understand I would see Him in my flesh. It was as if something was working on me to transform the all of me, but all too swiftly I lost contact again and again with this flash of insight and returned to my misery.

"'Then one day came Elihu, the young one, who with many fine words refuted my comforters' arguments and began to describe God in the way I was beginning to feel was nearer to my brief moments of understanding, but again, talk, talk, talk ...

"'I sat there and acknowledged that that was all I could do — stay there patiently in front of my unknowing. Stay there. Stay there ... until I began to feel I was being far more truthful than I had ever been before — that truly I *did not know*; that I *could not know anything about God*, which did not mean I did not believe in Him, but that I was nothing to Him, except when I acknowledged that I did not know him ... and emptiness came into me and I felt empty within and noticed that my sores were beginning to heal.

"'I saw then that three qualities were always in me, three contradictions absolutely necessary: very great doubt, very great faith, and very great perseverance, and that I was in fact sitting there, living all three.

"'I sat there with my very great doubt, my very great faith, my dogged perseverance and then ...

"'I saw Him.

"'I saw within me; saw His light, His sun, so bright and golden and heat-filled, so incomprehensible, immense, immortal that I called out to be taken away, far away and fast and at once, but then, I <u>heard</u> Him; heard the still small voice. Yes, small, not thundering, not loud, not angry; still, small, quietly asking *where were you Job when I laid the foundations of the earth? Who laid the cornerstone thereof when the morning stars sang together and all the Sons of God shouted for joy?*

"'I <u>saw</u> — within me. Immense light filled me, poured into me, and heat filled me so that my feet were like glowing coals and the blood flowed in my veins like molten lava. I felt visited by subtlety and beneficence and certitude.

"'And I began to feel that I was dissolving, my cells melting.

"'I saw no face, no form and yet before me a shape from which I heard a voice if it can be called by any word, be it voice, sound, vibration, and I sensed a loosening of my sinews, a releasing of my muscles, a losing of my form as if only in formlessness, however brief, could I face this vision, encounter it, see it without being struck down dead.

"'And out from the mightiness of this vision the grandeur of the voice — if voice it was — words whirled around me and within me: *Canst thou, Job, bind the sweet influence of the Pleiades, or loose the bands of Orion? Who hath put wisdom in the inward parts, or who hath given understanding to the heart?*'"

"This, then was our inheritance," said Jemima. "This is what our father, Job, taught us."

"The meaning of true suffering," said Kezia.

"Of the need", said Kerenheppuch, "for persistence in front of the height and the depth — the height which is God, the whole, and the depth which is my absorption in my little self — my fears, my concerns, my attachments, my desires, my cravings, my graspings ..."

"'The need for this encounter, this friction between those two opposites, this rubbing together of two sticks necessarily fierce in order to bring about fire, conflagration — a shift forward, a leap upward; that only the direct conflict between our real suffering and the real help can bring about the fire ...'"

"'To struggle valiantly not to be consumed, but to maintain silence in front of real suffering ...

"'To struggle valiantly to return again and again to a sense of myself here and now ...

"'To know that when I call, *Lord, Lord,* He will answer, *Here am I.*'

"That is what he told us ...

"That is what he handed down: very great doubt of oneself, of one's possibility to relate to the Whole on High; very great faith, very great perseverance; that there is no fixity; that we waver, we go far away; we return; that the faith contains the doubt and the perseverance; that real suffering had to be borne, undergone, then taken in hand and lived with as closely as one does if one is carrying something precious, or as one lives cheek by jowl with someone one does not always like ...

"He reminded us of the commandment of Moses — that near commandment to choose life over death, action over inertia in one's inner world just as one does in the outer world ...

"On many evenings we sat with him, sat close to our father, our old father and listened to him speaking thus.

"'I thought I knew,' he told us, 'but everything I thought I was experiencing, that I thought I was understanding was too far, too far from me — at a distant remove from the real presence. I saw that I had no choice but to wrestle with it, embrace it, allow this close encounter with the real presence, as close as the jugular vein, so close I no longer knew which was Him and which was me ... and that I was no longer allowed to go far away and return when I wished ... no, I had to be there all the time ... be there — that at the slightest attempt to leave I was pulled back to Him, to myself. That is terrible ... That is wonderful ...'

"'But, father,' we said, 'you would never have arrived at this place if you had not for all your life prayed according to your understanding, obeyed according to your understanding all the precepts, said all the prayers, practised all the practice ...'

"'No, children,' he murmured ... 'I suppose you may be right, but it was as if I had to reach the point of letting go, where I burst out with the words, *Eli, eli lama sabachtani* — *my God, my God, why hast thou forsaken me?* That until I was pierced by the sense of loss, of being abandoned, He could not come to me and I could not meet Him face to face; until I, my small person, decreased, He could not increase — that is what He needed from me. Until then, I had not known what real prayer was, real observance was: this persistent, direct, frequent experience of having to face suffering and Him again and again and again.'

"Sitting there with him, absorbing the life around us and listening to what he was transmitting to us, everything become as one — a large and lovely and laboured tapestry of sight, sound, colour, taste, joy and sorrow, of love, of longing ...

"That is what he handed down to us.

"And now we pass it on to you, dear Maryam, and you too, dear Elizabeth, for once again there will be born into our world another such man and also his wise and faithful harbinger ... yes, your sons ..."

"Our sons!"

Elizabeth turned to me, wide-eyed, pale, almost terror-stricken in her disbelief. She who had been married long and left her Zacharias these past three years to be with me for reasons which no-one yet had fully explained to her ...

And me? Likewise groping in the dark, only staying there because the trust I had in my mother was like a lamp, a bright candle ...

What were these daughters of Job telling us?

What was our destiny?

Why indeed had all these other women been summonsed by who knows what powers to tell us their stories?

That we should spend three years in this holy place did not seem so very strange — both our families were devout, observant, lovers of the Lord, wishing for us a sound grounding in what were women's tasks ...

And now Hannah, my mother, was looking at us both. One by one, slowly, slowly, her gaze full of immense tenderness, severity too — and sadness ... she began to speak:

"It is time," she said, "it is indeed time now to tell you both why you were asked to come here to Bethanehyeh ..."

Until now I had had the vaguest, rosiest dreams of marriage and motherhood, and I suppose I was expecting some sort of maternal homily about these things.

But no: by the time she had finished speaking I could not understand how I could ever have imagined that we were just being prepared, albeit particularly carefully, for the roles expected of any pious Hebrew woman.

No: by the time she had finished speaking I knew and understood fully and beyond the shadow of a doubt that Hannah, my mother, was Wisdom herself, Wisdom incarnate, *'mother of beautiful love, of awe, of knowledge and of holy hope.'*

Oh, my mother!

Taller than ever — like the cedar of Lebanon.

Straighter than ever — like the palm tree.

Stronger and sturdier than ever — like the old yet beautiful olive tree which grew at the heart of the most ancient of the groves around us.

Solar.

Lunar.

Stellar.

And there seemed to issue from her a wonderful fragrance — of the damask rose; of the frankincense they burn in the Temple on High Days and Holy Days; of another perfume, bittersweet, which — I was to recognise later, much later — was ... myrrh.

Oh, my mother!

Without her I would never have been able to carry a tithe of the sorrows and joys which were to be mine; never therefore have lived to hear Him murmur those same words, "Oh, my mother!" For yes, He was tender and loving to me; we did pray together, meditate together on the Silence in silence.

Oh, my mother!

Even as she began to speak, I should say, <u>because</u> of the way she spoke I was aware of a great space within me, an active emptiness ready to welcome the destiny she was describing.

She spoke in such a way and from such a high place in herself that any vestige of my girlish dreams were gently blown away by the soft warm air which was her voice — as the gently persuasive zephyr blows away the small clouds which had been trying to cover the sun.

There was nothing harsh in her tone, as she gazed at me with a look of the utmost humbleness and gravity and said:

"My child, we are in front of mystery far, far beyond our understanding. We are in front of mystery itself. We cannot explain mystery, but before we fall silent in front of it, I can describe the result of mystery, of what will come to pass in you and what will be born from you ..."

Of course she heard my gasp but barely paused:

"What will come to pass in you and what will issue from you will be nothing less than the growth and birth of a messenger from the Whole on High ..."

I had bowed my head, humbled, burdened, terrified, mystified ... when I heard a strange low sound, a moan ...

It was coming from one of the women.

I looked up, curious in spite of my own concern.

I looked up and heard Rebekah moan. "Ah!" she breathed. "The priest ... my two ... my twins ... is this what I was to understand? Is Two to become, at last, One?"

And she stared at me her eyes brimming with tears ...

I too now remembered what she had told us:

"We have now two sons in the womb of Rebekah ... but there will come a day when the two natures will no longer be at war with one another, but <u>reconciled in one form</u>, and form and emptiness will meet and dwell together"

Rebekah and I looked at one another and I nodded so slightly only she — and my mother, I am sure — saw ...

"We are in front of mystery," my mother was saying once again, "a mystery which it has been foretold will come from a virgin, a daughter of Yerushalayim - the inner Jerusalem of a woman able to transcend her own desires, her own small fate, in order to lay a foundation."

It was then immediately — and for the very first time — that I became aware of my womb as a place of joyful sensation. Far from the monthly cramping signals which all women know, I felt a piercing, a turning over, a fluttering. I knew I had moved to some new self — no longer puzzled, nor mystified, but joyful, accepting, relieved. At last! As if the holy curtains had been drawn back, I understood why really I was at Bethanehyeh! A quickening, you could say.

'Yes,' I cried. 'Yes' filled my womb! I do not think I cried out loud that 'Yes,' but I saw in my mother's eyes that she had heard my thoughts, felt my feelings, heard my 'yes' and so was able to continue.

"The spirit, the breath itself, of the Whole on High will be breathed onto you, into you — and a dove will appear, descending in a stream of light. You will be visited by an archangel and he will remain with you, full of tender mercies, while a great shadow will fall over you, to protect you, like a veil, from the power and the force coming down from above and into you. And during that time a holy thing will plant itself in you and begin to grow ...

"You have been prepared for this by the work we do here and in which you have been taking part ...

"We have worked here, we are working here to experience ecstasy — that energy, that inspiration, that breath of desire, that overflowing love of the Whole on High, that wish to be. joined with it ...

"We have worked here to let the ecstasy fill us with a sense of service; that all our actions, all our tasks are to be undertaken for their own sake and not for any fruits, and offered up in sacrifice. We make all our acts sacred, because they are filled with mindfulness and so have meaning ...

"We have worked here to arrive at the practice of the finest, deepest quality of prayer possible for us fallible creatures — prayer as intention. We struggle unceasingly to return to the prayer, not to abandon the prayer, to live the prayer, accepting again and again to be at risk — that risk which accompanies an active form of acquiescence in what is beyond our understanding, yet nevertheless *known* in our heart of hearts as real, as true ...

"Yes, dear child, of the four practices this one is to be your most necessary one.

"And lastly, we work daily on the demands of self. We die daily to the demands of self, self, self as the only way to arrive at true humility. We try constantly to put ourselves under something greater than ourselves ...

"And you see now, dear Maryam, if you look round at us, you are the only one here who is virgin — not only in the body sense, but also in spirit. You are strong enough, whole enough, prepared enough to carry fire, light; able, perhaps, to step closer to the Burning Bush than anyone except Moses. It is from your strong wholeness that a child will be born ..."

"A child ..."

I found that my hands were loosely clasped around my belly ...

"A child ... a holy thing?"

I looked up and found that the wisdom in my mother's face reflected in the faces of all those other women, who seemed, like her, to be grand in stature, composed, imbuing me with courage, understanding, love. I was not alone, I would not be alone in front of what was to come to pass through me ...

A child, I dreamed. A special child, a holy thing ... again my womb turned over; I trembled; I feared; I rejoiced; I dreamed a little of how it would feel to hold a baby in my arms ...

And then I came to and heard my mother speaking to Elizabeth:

"And you, dear, faithful cousin who have sacrificed three years of life without your beloved Zacharias — you too shall bear a child ..."

And here Elizabeth started up, fell back, first scarlet-faced, then ashen, dry-eyed, then tears pouring down like a joyful new spring gushing forth ...

"For the holy boy born from Maryam will most surely need a cousin — first as playmate and then as one prepared to go into the wilderness with him to prepare the way. Just as we have been here, preparing your way as well as Maryam's, so too will your sons, when *they* are thirteen, leave you, withdraw for many more years than you have spent here. For many more years, they are to prepare to appear in the world at the ripe time and in the right place to sow seeds of a new kind of kingdom. They will sow the seeds in men and women for that is the only place where this new kingdom can flourish. It will be a kingdom, not of ruling, nor reigning but offering a completely new possibility within us of attuning to a different kind of heaven. This will not be some other life after life, but here and now, attuning to a shimmering cosmic vibration linking them to the Whole on High ...

"And it is for this, Maryam, that your holy child will come into the world. He will show the way with stories, with gatherings among all manner of men and women, with miracles, bringing people back to life, making the blind to see and the lame to walk. He will not act to show off extraordinary powers, not do it for his own ends, but to show in an outer, visible form that it is not necessary to be dead in spirit while alive in the flesh. It is not necessary to be blind to inner vision even if eyes fail; to hobble and limp in one's inner attitude however lame the limbs may be ...

"He will often weep with the effort demanded; he will often feel alone, forsaken ... He will need first the strength of your son, Elizabeth. Your son will be strong — no reed blowing in the wind.

"Maryam's son will need friends, loyalty. He will have them — the first ones brought to him, again, dear Elizabeth, by <u>your</u> son.

"You, Maryam, will also have a helpmate — the good carpenter Joseph of Nazareth. He will marry you, shield you from those who will not understand your story. You two and Elizabeth and Zacharias will meet together, pray together, trust together and allow the path your sons must follow to be straight and unimpeded."

Elizabeth stared at me.

I stared at her.

And then, most surely reading our thoughts, Hannah, my mother, said:

"Yes, indeed. Enough. It is enough. Eva, Sarah, Rebekah! Leah, Rachel, Ruth! and you, Kezia, Jemima, Kerenheppuch, daughters of Job! Mothers, daughters, let us now dance! The time for words is over ... Let us dance that our bodies commit to the words, our hearts to the movement which will open us — which always opens us to being able to fulfil what is demanded of us ..."

I should have said long, long before this that, of course, we danced every day. Every day, in the late afternoon, when the great heat began to decline and the little evening breeze to rustle the olive leaves, we would go down to the grove — yes, the same grove where the visitors appeared and met with us ...

"Yes, indeed, come! Let us dance! Come! But before we do I have something to say to my namesake ..."

The voice was strong and clear.

It was Miriam, first on her feet, her tambour in her hand.

What could my mother say? There would, after all, be more words before the dance but she had to allow the great, the formidable prophetess to give voice just as she had to the others.

"I too am a mother," Miriam began. "I have born my son, Hur, from my womb, but who is to say whether I was more mother than sister to my brother, Moses? For when we heard the Pharaoh's edict — that all boy Hebrew babies were to be killed — my mother, the <u>mother</u> of Moses, just stood there frozen with fear and it was I who urged her to weave a basket of reeds and pitch and to lay her little son in it and entrust him to the waters of the Nile.

"And now here *we* are, cradled by the security of this special place, with the task of caring for you, nurturing you, sustaining you, preparing you for your great role — for you will be the womb for another kind of Moses, who heard the voice and obeyed it just as your son will.

"Yes, I am a mother like all these other mothers here. But I am also another kind of mother: a prophetess. And what does that mean? I see further ... I call ... I see what is necessary to awaken the dreamers, the sleep-walkers. Through me something is seen, something is called. Through me a new awareness is conceived and born — a movement from slavery and sleep towards freedom and awakening ...

"Before Moses was born I saw a strange radiance the house. Suddenly it was filled with the light of the sun, the light of the moon, and I knew then that this baby was destined to change the enslaved life of the Hebrews.

"As I pushed the cradle out into the water I knew the river flow would send it gently into that inlet where the Pharaoh's daughter always came down to bathe. I was the one who leapt up from our hiding place among the rushes and suggested my mother as a wet-nurse. I was the one who kept faith — not hope — that in time this brother of mine would rise up and lead us out of Egypt ... And why do you think I led the dance and the hymn of praise when we came to the other side of the Red Sea, if it was not to celebrate that there was no going back, but only a going forward towards that mountain, Sinai ... a higher place ... moving on and upwards to a vision of a new way ...

"You have heard the mothers' stories and now you are hearing mine. They all tell of being surprised by joy, afflicted with sorrow, broken by suffering ... Their hearts were broken — and hearts must be broken before we can care about the other — through their love for their children. But most of them also tell of their own dark acts. Sarah still feels guilt at the way she behaved towards Hagar; Rebekah for putting her cunning at the service of the Lord God's plan; Leah for conniving with her father's deceit; and even little Ruth — you saw how she blushed — even good Ruth had something to confess!

"And I? My dark act was to complain to the Lord God about my brother, Moses, because I was jealous of him — jealous that only he, not I, nor our priestly brother Aaron, ever came face to face with Him. For that I was punished, made leprous, threatened to be outcast if the children of Israel had not pleaded for me. The children of Israel, those restless, complaining, untrusting children whom Moses cajoled and admonished and cherished all those years in the wilderness ... those other children always loved me. They would not let my punishment be too harsh; would not move on without me, because they depended on the waters of my well, this wonder which followed us through all our days and nights in the wilderness.

"I grew jealous of him because of his wife, because he had a wife. I, the sister who had saved his life and led the dance, I could not bear that he loved another woman. I also could not bear that he had the ear of God in ways that I did not. These jealousies grew and festered in me slowly but steadily until the day I burst out with them and was punished. A necessary punishment, for I had to withdraw alone, apart from everyone in that desert wilderness. Alone in the wilderness so that I could be alone with myself and look at myself as in a mirror and see the ravages of this terrible disease, jealousy. Why should Moses not love and enjoy his wife? I had a husband I loved and who loved me; I was still his sister and he needed me. He needed me to help care for the children of Israel, and they needed me, the children needed me as their mother, and suddenly I saw that this was what I wanted most — to care for them and allow the waters to purify them, assuage their thirsts, cool them in the heat of the day, assuage their thirsts physical and spiritual as the manna from heaven assuaged their hungers physical and spiritual. Moses needed me if we were to help the Whole on High to bring these children up the mountain, where their vision and understanding would widen and broaden and they could shake off the last tatters of their inner and outer slavery.

"See, then, Maryam, how we have all struggled to reconcile the light with the dark for you. You are the result of this reconciliation striven for over many thousands of earth's years ..."

"And the result of love," came the voice of my mother, Hannah.

"The four loves my daughter is imbued with, working in her from the first day that the angels had her in their charge — the love of God, the love of service, the love of prayer, the love of humility ..."

I welcomed the interruption, the voice calm yet vibrant with warmth and steadfastness.

"And indeed, of love," the prophetess agreed.

"Thank you, Miriam," said my mother.

She turned to Eva, copper-haired and beautiful, copper-haired and dignified, full-breasted, broad of hip, strong, sinuous, who had endured so much calumny and has continued to do so just as in time that dark and faithful friend of Yeshua would do so, patiently carrying a heavy burden of misunderstanding till the end of time.

"Eva!" said my mother. "Eva! Mother of all living. As much source of life as water is. Indeed, the very source, there at the beginning of the manifestation of the hidden, at the beginning of the necessary descent before the necessary return which we are here now to help to bring about! We salute you!

"Sarah! Rebekah! Leah! Rachel! We salute you, the first mothers, keepers of the home, the hearth, the heart's centre. We salute you and honour you, the first four pillars of the canopy that shelters and nurtures the bodies and the souls within them, who went about their work daily and faithfully, making it possible for the men to go about *their* work ...

"And Ruth, Jemima, Kezia, Kerenheppuch! We salute and honour you also, virtuous women, whose price is above rubies, who see to their households, sustain their men, cherish the children, carefully. Let us all rise up now and join Miriam in the dance ..."

To the beat of Miriam's tambour and the cadence of our own singing, we danced first in a circle, each with our right hand on the right shoulder of the one in front — slowly at first, but little by little, faster, faster, all reversing the direction at a certain moment, the circle to hallow all the parts of our bodies, to melt our cells, and, through the beat of our feet and the lifting of our heels above the dry earth dust, lifting ourselves up, up towards that whole, that Presence, allowing it to spread itself about us, over us, among us, upon us; the circle which has neither end or beginning, timeless. And because the singing and the dancing were linked by a profound spiritual intention, our little selves could not but fall from us as leaves fall from a tree. And because our little selves fell from us and we experienced a kind of dissolving, it was true to say that the Whole on High, the Word, came down through the dance, into the material world and made itself felt.

And when we had danced thus for a while we began to dance the pattern, the pattern of the four worlds, the four worlds of the Tree of Life, of the Sefirot, those ten bejewelled keys to the nature of the Whole on High.

With heads bowed, arms outstretched, one palm turned upwards, the other downwards, we turned and turned, travelling through the jewels of the Tree, zig-zagging through it like a lightning flash, affirming as we turned each precious name, each attribute of God:

Keter, Hokmah, Binah, Daat;

Hesded, Din, Tiferet;

Netzah, Hod, Yesod

Malkhut

Crown, wisdom, understanding, <u>knowledge</u>;

Mercy, rigour, <u>beauty</u>;

Eternity, reverberation, <u>foundation</u>;

<u>Kingdom</u>.

Yes, by stepping into our appointed and practised places we began to make the worlds turn. How I loved to be part of helping the worlds turn. I danced for many, many years after we left that special place, until my spine began to stiffen and I had to accept to give my place to a younger woman and join the crones who sit and try by their inner attitude and inner posture to represent the verticality which is the axis, whether moving or sitting — the still point from which all else moves and manifests.

But that day when we danced was unique. Hitherto we had danced daily with the other women living at Bethanehyeh. We had till then never danced with our visitors ...

And it was not Miriam who led the dance — yes, she stood up first and with her tambour and yes, she took the first step, but in fact it was Grace who led that dance, grace in the form of Hannah, my mother.

After we had danced the pattern of the Tree of Life, we returned to our circle and with Grace, with Hannah, my mother, standing in its centre we began to sing 'Amens' to all her invocations. Broken phrases issued from her, utterances: *Holy, holy, holy; praise to the holiest in the height and in the depths be praise; breathe on us breath of God: Amen, Amen, Amen,* and other heartfelt submissions too intimate to reveal here.

That day the Whole on High took part in our dancing and would again on a far off night on the Mount of Olives in Yerushalayim.

*****

'On the Mount of Olives in Yerushalayim ...'

How those words freeze my hand, my mind, my heart! So much so that I find I cannot go on with my story.

The old priest, Simeon, who had waited to see my son, Yeshua, had warned me as he held the baby in his frail arms, that a sword would pierce my heart. And indeed it has taken every second, every minute, every hour of the long years of my life, now drawing to an end, to try to absorb my destiny, digest it, acknowledge it, appreciate it, and put my immense joy and my immense suffering to good use for <u>all</u>. I do not begrudge the cost. I rejoice that men, women and their children turn to me as mother. My heart is now so broken, so tender, so large; my arms wide enough to embrace entirely this world. Daily I breathe love into its atmosphere.

But now, in front of trying to describe what happened after Bethanehyeh, I find I cannot do it.

I cannot ...

Jenny Koralek

PART THREE - ELIZABETH
I

'How can a man know what a woman's life is?

...The man spends a night by a woman and goes away. His life and body are always the same. The woman conceives. As a mother she is another person than the woman without a child. She carries the fruit of the night for nine months in her body. Something grows. Something grows into her life that never again departs from it. She is a mother. She is and remains a mother even though her child die ... For at one time she carried the child under her heart. And it does not go out of her heart ever again. Not even when it is dead'.

(Words of an Ethiopian woman recorded by Leo Frobenius, the anthropologist, and quoted by C Kerenyi in his *Kore* in *Essays on a Science of Mythology, The Myth of the Divine Child and the Mysteries of Eleusis*)

She could not continue ... And we left it there. I understood. Too hard to re-live what she had been through; too hard to translate into words.

But now, these long years later, she's gone, and I, a poor enough interpreter, feel I must try to finish the tale in my more ordinary way. I admit I feel the burden of this, and will try to tell it as best I can and with very great respect.

Yes, she's gone.

Maryam, my cousin.

Maryam.

She's gone.

I saw her go.

He came for her Himself.

Of course He came for her Himself to lift her up to her rightful place beside Him — the mother who had borne Him, borne His life, borne His death; accepted the destiny intended for her from before she was born; submitted to the teachings of angels, suffered the force of their energy, always demanding from her ever more emptying of her small Maryam self.

A young girl, a young girl who could count on her fingers the times spent girlishly — at the well in the evening, at the ribbon stall, at the bangle sellers in the bazaar on rare holidays ... who certainly never giggled behind the veil drawn across her face when the boys passed by with their goats and sheep ...

A young girl who, if she had not been prepared, would never have withstood that mysterious overshadowing announced to her by an archangel ...

She was married to Joseph the carpenter almost as soon as we left that place of preparation ... Joseph a much younger man than my Zacharias, whatever I hear now being told. He was not an old man, but not a youth either: a widower, good, hard-working, carefully chosen by the priests of the Temple.

I still hold in passionate vivid memory that blest visit.

I was nearer to my time than she was and, being older, tired easily. I remember still how tenderly she led me to the shade beneath the ilex tree outside my little house and set me on a stool, leaning over me to rub my aching back.

I remember too how my dear Zacharias smiled upon us on his way to his devotions and his duties in the Temple ... He was dumb then, you know. And remained dumb until our Jochanan was born. Dumb because he did not believe the voice he heard one day at his prayers in the Temple, the voice which told him I would after all bear a son, the voice of an angel messenger.

It seems we were surrounded by them from the beginning, as we struggled to trust these messages, that we were all being called to play our parts in a mystery.

Yes, Zacharias smiled upon us that day. He was happy, that man of good faith; dumbstruck, but I sensed he was happy to be so. Later, when he could speak again, he never used words overmuch for the rest of his days, as if he had learned how unnecessary so many of them are.

I never told him what Maryam told me that day. It was early in the day, as she still rose (as I did all the days of my life) at dawn, always at dawn, just as we had at Bethanehyeh, to watch the sun rise, and then went about the daily tasks while Joseph was over at his workshop.

"I was sitting as usual, spinning the Temple threads when I heard it — that sound I had not heard since I was a child — that rushing mighty sound like the beating of great wings and there, kneeling, was this presence...

"I too fell to my knees, bowed my head, heard the voice.

"*'Hail, Maryam, blessed Maryam, the Whole on High is with you. Do not be afraid...'*

"Only then did I dare look up and seeing the gravity on the face, felt not fear, but unworthiness, and made a move away from the presence and sensed my hand beginning to move as if to fend off the demand I knew was coming ...

"*'Fear not ... you will conceive a child, a son who shall be great, a new kind of king of a new kind of kingdom ...'*

"'But,' I murmured ...

"*'Trust'*, came the answer.

"*'This holy thing will be the incarnation, the meeting place of high and low, no longer separated, but One. All that has gone before comes together now in your womb ... All that you have learned and loved is in your blood, your breath, your cells and in your marrow bone, and will pass through you to the child. Let the silence do its work upon you and within you, and all will come to pass as it has been foretold and prepared since the day Adam became two and stepped out of Paradise ...'*

"At these words I felt my refusal fall from me and I heard myself say, 'Amen. So be it.' And it was then that he told me that <u>you</u> too, my dear cousin, were also carrying a child and even as I smiled with delight and opened my mouth to rejoice, the presence was suddenly gone."

"Did you tell Joseph? What did he say?" I asked.

"He just said, 'I know, and I will take care of you,' and then we wept together a strange mixture of joyful and sorrowful tears."

By now I was overcome. I rose to my feet and it was then that I felt my child quickening — a flutter so light like a tiny pat on the cheek, so swift that I almost did not believe in it, and I felt myself filled with life and with a great love for Maryam and the holy thing in her womb, and I heard myself say in a voice I did not know was mine, loud and clear, "Oh, Maryam! Full of grace! Blessed art thou among women, and blessed is the fruit of thy womb and blessed am I that you have come to me and told me this great news, that you are to be the mother of my Lord!"

As I said the words, once again my baby leapt in my womb as if with joy, and then Maryam began to sing — not one of our familiar hymns of praise from Bethanehyeh, but a song of broken words which seemed to form itself at that very moment: *I magnify the Lord for he has done me great things and holy is his name ... Fire in my soul ... light everywhere ...* and then she broke off singing and said to me: "All I am really trying to say is *Yes.*"

And burst into tears.

PART THREE - II

'The individual ego is the stable in which the Christ-child is born.'

'We are no more than the manger in which the Lord is born.'

(C G Jung)

I was not there when He was born.

That was in Bethlehem, not so far from where we were living, but I had not long given birth to my Jochanan and was still quite weak and weary. It was a bitter winter and Zacharias forbade me to make the journey. Bethlehem was far from their home town of Nazareth. They had been obliged to travel there not long before the baby was due, all for the sake of some new tax census.

It was Joseph who later told me most about it all ...

"It was a long journey and slow," he said, "the roads being narrow and crowded, so we should not have been surprised to find that all the inns were full, but we were, and anxious too, as Maryam's pains were beginning and she could hardly sit a moment longer on the donkey. Then at the last place where we tried for a room the innkeeper's wife could see what was going on and showed us to a kind of animal shelter in a cave among the rocks.

"'Lift me down,' my dear girl begged. So I lifted her down and laid her on some straw lying in the cave and then I grew afraid. I did not know what to do, and, if you can believe it, I ran out of the cave, foolishly hoping to find someone, a woman who would help her. I should tell you that it was twilight, and the stars were beginning to appear ...

Jenny Koralek

"I heard Maryam cry out once and, as I turned to run back to her I saw that everything had come to a standstill — everything. The air froze, there was no wind, the stars seemed larger than usual but did not twinkle. I saw a bird or two unmoving though in full flight towards their night-time roost. I saw a shepherd in the distance with sheep still as stone. The shepherd had his staff raised but could not bring it down upon their backs ... It only lasted a few seconds but I knew that in that frozen moment the child had been born ... A little breeze blew again, the stars twinkled, the sheep pushed against one another and ran on as the shepherd's staff smote them and then suddenly the sky was filled with a great light and out of that great light a huge star appeared, outshining all the others put together. The light was particularly strong over that cave stable. I heard the shepherd calling to his mates and a crowd of them appeared all looking upwards and pointing, and then I did indeed see a woman coming towards me. She was holding her hands to her face, weeping and smiling both.

"'It has happened!' she cried out to me as she drew closer. At first I thought it was a question and a strange one at that but then I understood she was telling me: 'It has happened! At last! And I am here! I, Eva, mother of all living ... Called back now to bear witness that the descent is over at last, and after the descent the return ...'

"Just as a few moments before the universe had stood still, now it was my turn. All my ordinary thoughts and understanding were replaced by some bright vision I knew was not from my own mind and would not last, but I seemed to know that this was not some dream but that we were all for this while outside time ... and it seemed quite natural that Eva should be here and now asking me so humbly — asking me, *the carpenter from Nazareth*, if she could enter the cave with me and see the babe and the mother with her own eyes ...

"I bowed to her and led her into the cave and there I beheld my dear Maryam holding the child in her arms, wrapt in some profound experience, her head bowed, and quiet and still in a way I would not have thought possible for a woman who had just been in labour to give birth and all alone.

"After a while she looked up, but as if blind to our presence, looked up above us as if she were listening to a voice we could not hear ...

"'Yes,' she was whispering. 'Yes ... Yes ...'

"And then her vision must have faded for she suddenly saw us.

"'It has happened,' she said softly. The same words as Eva's. 'It has happened. I have been overshadowed, the babe has been overshadowed by a great force, as the angel foretold. The shadow was dark but the force was light itself. I felt both enter us both ... and His name is Yeshua.'

"And then she astonished me by turning towards my companion saying, 'Eva! Eva! I knew you would come.' And she smiled and held out the babe to Eva.

"Eva took the sweet child so carefully, so tenderly into her cradling arms that tears came to my eyes.

"Then she laid the boy again in His mother's arms and with her arm around Maryam I heard her say, 'As I told you long ago in that special place, our tasks go together ... as I came into being to assist the falling into form so you came into being to assist in the rising, the ascent, the return to formlessness, which is oneness. I rejoice today; my burden has lessened and I will never be far from you as yours grows heavier.'

"I was shocked to hear these words, but even more shocked by the look which passed between the two women, of acknowledgement, of shared *knowledge* or acquaintance with and acceptance of grief or some suffering already foreseen. And then Eva vanished and I ran forward to embrace my wife and gently touch the baby's head with my large fingers.

"I felt I had been witness to some great mystery in which it seemed I had been called to play a humble, obedient, undemanding part."

"Yes," I interrupted Joseph.

He stared at me and said, "You too? You are part of this?"

"Yes," I said. "And like you, it is hard and will be even harder to be onlookers ..."

He shook his head in bewilderment and then straightened and said, simply, "I will take care of her and, insofar as it is possible, of Him as long as I live ..."

And we embraced in silence.

"But I have not finished telling the tale," Joseph then said.

"Those shepherds I had seen in the distance pointing at the star and calling to one another excitedly were now heading towards the cave. They shuffled about shyly in the entrance until we beckoned them to come in. They fell to their knees and stared and stared at the child now surrounded, as Maryam was, by this great light, and then without saying a word got up and shuffled away. During the next few days they would return often, sometimes with their wives and children, and later other local people came. They never spoke, but stared and stared and often their faces began to lose the look of strain and fatigue which comes with too much work, too little sleep and not enough to eat.

"On the seventh day after the birth, when there was a small crowd of these poor people around the cave's entrance, a clamour arose and we all heard the clop of camel hooves. They started turning and looking, then made way for three grand men, richly clothed. They looked like kings or great lords, but dusty and weary as if they had come a long, long way. Later I learned that they were not kings, but astrologers, sages from Babylon, who had all been following and studying the sudden appearance and movement of this great star. They had made their way to Jerusalem and started asking where might be the new anointed one, the new *maschiach*. 'We have seen his star appear in the first rays of the dawn.' They told me that in their ancient books the birth of this child had long been foretold. 'At times when mankind is losing its way, losing its contact with the Whole on High,' they were to tell me, 'a messenger is sent from Above to remind them of what in their hearts they know, but have forgotten, and all the signs we have been studying seem to show that this child is just such a messenger.' Then they told me of another such messenger, born five hundred years ago in some country far to the East of ours. They called him Bud ... Buddha, I think it was, and described him as the Awakened One ...

"I shudder as I tell you this, for I feel the mystery, but it is beyond me. You must see me as an idiot that I do not understand the meaning of all that is taking place in front of my very eyes. But I am a simple man, a plain man, obeying the demand of the priests who chose me to take Maryam as my wife and to take care for her without ever explaining why. They looked at me so seriously, with such trust, as if they were confident that I could play my small part decently. For all I know they too were simply obeying some call without knowing its full purpose.

"Truth to tell, Elizabeth, I know and I don't know; sometimes I glimpse understanding that something truly mysterious is afoot; then I lose sight of it. I have decided to accept my place without question ..."

He paused and then said, "Of course, I have had dreams, you know ..."

"Of angels perhaps?" I asked.

"How do you know that?"

"I just wondered ... I have met others who had been visited by angels ..."

"Yes, but these were just *dreams* of angels, once or twice, talking to me, and in the dreams I understand what they are telling me, but when I wake up, I have forgotten.."

We did not speak for a while. It did not seem right to urge him to say more than he wished.

When he did speak again he picked up the story.

"These astrologers brought very precious gifts: gold, frankincense and myrhh, which they laid at Maryam's feet as she sat there with the baby in her arms. At the time I was mystified but after they had spoken with me I could at least see that if the child really *is* a messenger from on High then surely He is a sort of king, and gold, we know, is a gift for kings; frankincense, the purest incense is burnt in the Temple as an offering to the Lord God, and myrhh we had heard was burnt at the head and the foot of the high and mighty as they lay dead and in their shrouds ...

"Yes, the sight of those pale amethyst crystals made me tremble. We were joyfully celebrating a birth and yet something to do with death had already entered the cave along with shepherds, sheep, astrologers, and, I forgot to say, an ox and a donkey whose warm damp breath took the edge off the chill, and their chomping jaws, clattering movements as they shoved up against each other, just about helped to keep things ordinary ..."

"Did they stay long, those sages?" I asked.

"No, no," said Joseph. "They left rather suddenly after a young fellow appeared and took them off a distance. He seemed to be telling them something alarming, because when he had gone they packed up their things, saddled their camels, made most solemn and courteous farewells and left. I noticed they did not go back the way they had come, and only later did I understand why. Apparently when they first went to Jerusalem and started asking about the whereabouts of the child, Herod himself got wind of this and panicked at the thought that a new king had been born who would be a threat to him. He was courteous to the visitors and invited them to feel free to continue their search, but to be sure and come back and tell him when they had found the 'king' so that he too could come and pay his respects ..."

We looked at one another, nodding with the understanding of hindsight and close to tears.

"There is one last thing I must tell you," he went on. "About the baby's circumcision. Here again I feel the dimness of my understanding. We took Him to the little temple in Bethlehem, and at the end of the ceremony, when the poor child was wailing and Maryam struggling to soothe him by putting him to the breast, an old priest came forward from a dark corner and humbly asked if he might look at the child. He came close and peered at the baby, by now calming and settling to sleep with little tears on his pale cheeks. And then suddenly this old man burst out 'Yes! This is the one! This is most surely the one!' And he started singing a holy sounding song, something like, *Lord, now I may depart in peace. I have waited long for this day and now I have seen with my own eyes — the new man, the incarnation of thy word* ...

"He took one of the child's feet in his large old hand and bent and kissed it. And then! Then he looked at Maryam with such kindness and pity, and said something which I could see terrified her: *This child is set for the fall and rising of many ... and a sword shall pierce through thine own soul also.* Then he touched Maryam gently, oh so gently on the arm and, bowing to me, he shuffled away ..."

Joseph told me all these things in the days after our arrival in Egypt where we had had to take sudden refuge when the baby was not much more than one week old.

Yes, I went with them. I and my little son, by then nearly a year old.

For as soon as we heard of Herod's evil decree — that all boys under the age of two must be found and killed — we knew we must leave the country immediately. At the time we had no idea what the dreadful reasoning might be for such a decree, but we did not wait to find out. Zacharias met Joseph as dusk fell and before moonrise we were on our way — Maryam, Joseph, the two babies and me.

My dear, devout and foolish Zacharias! He would not leave the temple. He would not leave the temple. "I'll be all right," he insisted. "They are not looking for old greybeards! It will blow over and you will be back before you know it."

And he kissed us tenderly and turned away homewards.

I thank the Lord God that I did not know then that they would kill my Zacharias.

Kill my Zacharias.

Kill my good, pious Zacharias, because he would not tell them where I was hiding with Jochanan.

I thank the Lord God that I passed those years in Egypt not knowing that the father would never know the son. Later, of course, much later, I would thank the Lord God that Zacharias had not lived first to be proud and mystified by him only to lose him, as I was to lose him, to the same kind of blood-stained vengeance as that which killed him.

It had never crossed our minds in our hurry and flurry that he might be in danger. Someone, out of fear must have told the soldiers that Zacharias, old as he looked had recently fathered a son. But I never went back to our home near that temple. I stayed always near to Joseph and Maryam, and found solace in the friendship that grew between our sons.

But on that dark night when we fled to Egypt we just slipped away as lightly laden as possible so as not to tire the donkeys. Poor Joseph! He ran back and forth between us, urging the animals on. We made do with as little food as we could and carrying precious water in a few leathern pouches, and using little known paths, we eventually came to the old Way of the Land of the Philistines, that ancient caravan route from King Solomon's times which would take us down into Egypt.

We were on the road for over three weeks. By day we hid in caves and slept, travelling only by night. The danger seemed less the nearer we got to Gaza, but we took no risks and did not emerge in broad daylight until we were well over the border. We did not settle anywhere until we came to a town where travellers from many lands mingled and marketed. Here Joseph had no trouble in finding work, and we lodged quietly and lived quietly in a narrow crowded street. Maryam and I found work too, spinning for one of the many weavers of carpets and cloth, which we could do from home, sitting in the doorway to get the best of the daylight while Jochanan took his first steps and Yeshua began to sit up in his little cradle and look about him.

But at night when the children were asleep we wept. We wept for all those innocents massacred because of Herod's terrible fear of his power being usurped by a new ruler. We wept and Joseph's face darkened in anger, sorrow and sympathy.

I think those were the days when even Maryam's faith and determination to serve the purpose for which she had been born, and for which she had been prepared, weakened and threatened to disappear altogether.

I think now that this was the first of Maryam's many great sorrows.

"I feel so guilty and so helpless," she sobbed in my arms more than once. "It is bad enough that you should be parted for who knows how long from Zacharias because of my child and then I think of all those little ones ... and the mothers ... all those mothers ..."

More than once I tried to comfort her — and myself — saying again and again, "We can only pray that these children we have borne will indeed bring in their different ways the promise of help and love and light and joy, which we have been given to understand is the purpose of their coming into life on this earth ..."

And I would try to reassure her that this would indeed come to pass, but we both knew that she would carry forever the burden of the knowledge of those deaths. I think it strengthened our resolve to prevent harm befalling our sons so that they would grow up to fulfil their tasks.

Our solace was the joy our babies gave us. Our going down into Egypt was a return to the ordinary, which I know, even through my grief, I welcomed. Secretly I could not help wondering if it was the same for Maryam.

Joseph certainly seemed to welcome a return to normality, his hand once more firmly on his saw. Perhaps we were all hiding behind the hurly burly of keeping house, earning our bread, scrubbing our clothes on the flat stones by the cistern, listening to the other women's gossip and hoping they would not demand tittle-tattle from us, mingling with crowds in the *souk*, watching from our doorstep while Yeshua toddled after Jochanan and tried to join in his cousin's games with the other children. Yes, our time in Egypt was the happiest, a deep immersion into the dense and dreaming world of matter. It was necessary for both our sons — a necessary baptism into the humdrum if they were to be accepted one day as men among other men, and not as remote ascetics who had no understanding of hardship, toil, sickness and doubt, as well as all the joys, moments of tenderness, kindness which make up all lives.

PART THREE - III

'Consider the lilies of the field: they toil not neither do they spin, yet Solomon in all his glory was not arrayed like one of these ...'

These words I heard many years after our return from Egypt, spoken by Yeshua when He was teaching, but I use them here as they came to me when I was casting around how to describe the ten years or so of our lives in Nazareth after the death of Herod. And as I recite them to myself now I feel how what He said was, almost always, grounded in and inspired by the images of the natural world, which surrounded him, and the experiences he lived during those childhood years.

Our boys were four and nearly five years old when we decided it was safe to go home and those years until they left us remain with me as gentle, fruitful and ordinary. After the deserts we had travelled through, and the noisy town we had lived in, it was a joy to find ourselves in the green and pleasant land where Nazareth lies. It was delightful to have figs at our door and pomegranates in the little yard, where we hung our clothes out to dry. It was pleasant at Sabbath's end to walk past fields of cyclamen and anemones, down towards the date groves or past the vineyards heavy in September with dark grapes. The town was always filled with the life-giving smell of wood shavings and the noise of the saw and the plane against wood, the mild clatter of furniture being stacked for sale, the not so mild curses at nails dropped and hammers hitting thumbs.

Yeshua and Jochanan went to the priests for teachings and to learn Hebrew. They kept themselves a little apart from the other boys, but not enough to be disliked. They joined in games, they listened to problems and often solved them. Girls admired them shyly from a distance.

We were lulled, I see now. Lulled into a false sense that perhaps all that had gone before were dreams. We had stepped out into the real world.

But of course this was wishful imagining.

A day came when Yeshua vanished. Disappeared.

Maryam was distraught; Joseph angry because he could not bear to see her upset. Jochanan joined the search ... He had been out in the far fields that day, but I was accustomed to his frequent brief absences, which seemed to stem from a deep need for solitude.

Had Yeshua come to harm cutting wood in the old olive grove? Had he been bitten by a serpent? Had he taken sick of a sudden fever? Had he fallen in one of the rocky dry river-beds the men often used as short cuts to their work among the fruits of the field?

Towards the end of a long day Maryam and Joseph found him in the dark coolness of our little temple, deep in talk with our priest and three others visiting from Jerusalem no less.

I did not join them for the evening meal, feeling they needed to be alone, but next day as Maryam and I were grinding flour together I saw her red eyes, and found the courage to ask her what had happened.

She was silent for a long time, her hands still over the grain. Then wiping the damp hair from her tear filled eyes she said, "It has begun. Yesterday. It has begun ..."

"Begun?"

"When we reproached him, when we told him how worried we had been; when we asked why hadn't he told us where he was going for the first time in his life he grew angry — well no, not angry so much as strong and stern ... And then he just said, 'Mother, surely you know, you of all people, that I must soon now be about my father's business ...'

"Of course I knew he did not mean Joseph's business ... No, I knew what he meant and *you*, Elizabeth, you know too. How could we have been so nearly able and, I fear, willing to forget what we were being prepared for all those years ago? How could I not remember? How could I somehow have ceased to take it seriously?"

She sat back on her heels and clasped her hands in her lap.

I did likewise.

Suddenly two women in the midst of the lowly necessary task of preparing bread for baking, were called to prayer right there and then.

Emptying. Letting go. Accepting. Allowing the breath of YHVH to flow throughout our bodies, our cells, quickening our blood, saturating the marrowbone.

And then behind me and facing his mother, Yeshua's voice, still the soft voice of a boy not yet thirteen.

May Thy will be done.

Here am I, Abba, Father.

"And I," I heard Maryam say firmly, looking into her son's eyes.

Then I heard my own voice saying, "And I."

Dear mother, dear cousin.

Then, All shall be well. All, all shall be well ...

And so it came to pass.

The day after their bar-mitzvahs a tall, serious looking man all robed in white, appeared at the door.

The boys picked up the small bundles they had prepared the night before. Maryam and I handed them water-skins and pomegranates, kissed them lightly. Did not cling. Did not wail. Did not weep.

And away they went without looking back.

*****

We did not see them again for twenty years and when we did we found ourselves face to face with the transformation of two young boys into two lean, sun-browned, grave, quiet men, severe even, yet still tender towards their mothers.

But there was a depth about their gravity, a weight to it which might well have intimidated had we had not spent those years in Bethanehyeh.

We knew that they too had risen daily before the sun rose and in silence gathered with others, their faces turned towards the sun, offering up their hymn of praise for a new day; they too had then taken themselves off to work until the mid-day meal, stopping always to wash and change into their white robes, and then to eat gratefully a simple meal, a little loaf of bread, some vegetables, some fruit, always in silence before changing again into rough clothes and working till evening; they too had been living — but for far, far longer than we had — that concentrated daily practice of true prayer, inner labours married to outer labours, action and contemplation brought together, which can lead to a gradual growth in holiness.

But now they sat us down — the two mothers. (I should say that dear Joseph had been dead for over ten years by the time they returned).

They sat us down after the first evening meal we prepared for them, not at the door beneath the stars, but in the innermost room away from prying eyes and ears.

We sat for a long time in silence, turning inwards and back towards those special places we had all lived in.

Then Yeshua said quietly, "I have come to bring into being a new kind of kingdom, a new kind of heaven ..."

"Yes, this kingdom of heaven is now at hand, and I am ready now to prepare the way for it," Jochanan added, firmly, strongly, looking at Yeshua with an expression of such love and admiration I knew in that moment that all our hearts were going to be broken, that we were all going to be broken open utterly in order for some great birth to take place ...

Joy and anguish. Joy and anguish. I would not until that moment have believed it was possible to feel both at the same time.

I looked at Maryam. Was it the same for her? If so, she hid it well and asked calmly, but also a little coldly, "Tell us of this new kingdom ..."

"Possibility," said Yeshua. "It is about a new kind of possibility, the place and space in us for an ascent to begin, an ascent, a return to Wholeness. Nothing to do with the powers of kingship, of ruling, of reigning. No, this kingdom is interior, within us, within you, mother, and you, cousin Elizabeth, within Jochanan here and within me ... within all men, all women ..."

"You are talking of the possibility we experienced at Bethanehyeh, and which you have clearly also experienced in the community in which you have been living these past years," said Maryam. "But what of those many who have not had this help?"

"I am here to show the way," said Yeshua. "And I will call others to work with me ..."

He stopped because he saw that his mother was weeping.

"Mother?" he asked gently. "What is it?"

"All those innocent babes. All that anger and rage and jealousy ... for nothing ... for nothing ... All because one man, one king feared you had come to take his power from him ... All that bloodshed for *nothing*."

She wiped her eyes with her apron and turned on her son, almost angrily. "And who is to say that it will not happen again? If one man can so misunderstand your meaning, the reason for your existence, how can you be so sure that others there will understand any better what this new kingdom is? How can you be sure that more blood will not flow? More misunderstandings arise?"

"I cannot be sure," said Yeshua. "I cannot be sure, but I must try. I must obey what I have heard. This call. This acquaintance I have with another kind of kingdom in myself, another kind of heaven, not hereafter, but now, here and now, again and again, here and now ..."

And then He got up, crossed the room and knelt at His mother's feet. He took her hand and kissed it and said, "Oh, mother, my mother! Do not forget what you know and understand! Do not abandon me! You gave me breath. You are my atmosphere! Your love is in my marrow bone!"

"I will never abandon you, my son!" said Maryam, taking His hand and pressing it to her cheek. "I will never abandon you, but I will falter ... I will sometimes falter ..."

"Oh mother!" He replied. "And do you think that I will not?"

Then Maryam said, "And the heaven? Your heaven?"

"A vibration which dissolves form ..." said Yeshua.

"Is that it?" said Maryam joyfully. "Is that it? For I have met that many times at daybreak and day's end ..."

"I know that, my mother," said Yeshua who was still kneeling at Maryam's feet.

And if I were to try for a thousand years I could not tell anyone all that most surely passed between them then in one long, long look ...

At last Maryam bent and put her arms round her son's neck and kissed him and I heard Him say, "Holy Maryam, you will always be my beloved mother, mother *of a child caught up unto God*, but the day is coming when you will be the new Eva, the Eva *clothed in the sun, and the moon under her feet.*"

Maryam shook her head, but Yeshua just smiled, stood up and took his place again.

To my surprise I now found my voice and heard myself say, "And as you go about your work, what will you need from us?"

"There is another Bethanehyeh," said Yeshua. "A Bethanehyeh in the very midst of the noise of the world. Not far from Jerusalem, and a family there waiting to welcome you both and find you a dwelling close to their door. And I will come there very often. We need you to be near us once again as you were all the days of our childhood.

"We need you to be near us, but even more we need you to join us, to be our first followers, to listen to us and to remember what you hear as witnesses to what will come to pass ...

"We need you so that people see that you are not only the mothers who gave us birth, but the first spiritual mothers of a new kind of family we hope to create out of all the men, women and young ones who have ears to hear and eyes to see ..."

*****

Jochanan baptised Yeshua in the Jordan.

We were there, on the edge of the crowd — the first crowd in the north of the country come to see my son who, I had not long learnt, had been preaching and teaching far to the south from the day he came back into our world. And it seemed that whenever he was asked who he was, and what he was doing he would reply mysteriously, *I am the voice of one crying in the wilderness, Make straight the way of the Lord, as said the prophet Isaiah.*

Isaiah, no less. Everyone knew Isaiah, who had spoken of a time when the lion would lie down with the lamb and all would be led by a child, although at other times he spoke of a man of sorrows and acquainted with grief, who would be scorned and denied as an Anointed One ...

So we were there the day my son baptised Yeshua with the water of the river Jordan. It filled me with pride. I was there, but I saw only that, nothing more. Maryam was there and she saw what I saw, but she saw more.

"Look!" she whispered as Jochanan finished with the water.

"Where?"

"There! Up there! Above Yeshua's head. Don't you see it — that great light?"

"No," I said sadly.

"And I hear a sound ... can you hear it too, Elizabeth?"

"Just the noise of the crowd ..."

"No, this is something else ... perhaps it is inside me, I don't quite know ... almost a voice, a murmur, an affirmation of this moment ... ?"

"I do not hear it," I said.

"I hear it, I feel it ..." Maryam broke off and turned to me with an expression I had never seen before, but which I came to know as awe. It is beyond fear, and stops us in our tracks in front of the doorway to the love we seek to feel for the Whole on High, and challenges us to open it ...

But that day I did not understand anything very much, so I sighed and accepted that it was my place to remain at Maryam's side, ready to hold her up in body or in spirit. Slowly, from that day on, I began to ponder on what it really meant to support another, to help another. I came to experience and suffer, bear the seeming helplessness of helping; to learn that silence was needed, and a certain stolid persistence — grim even sometimes; a refusal to abandon, to give up that role. And at my best I sometimes understood it meant simply to *be* — *to be there with* the other ...

Jenny Koralek

PART THREE - IV

'And the third day there was a marriage in Cana of Galilee; and the mother of Jesus was there'.

Not long before we left Nazareth there was a wedding in nearby Cana.

The groom was a childhood friend of Jochanan and Yeshua's so of course we were all invited. Jochanan had stayed only a few more days at home with us after the baptism, but during that time you could say he gave two of his most ardent followers to Yeshua. One was called Andreas, the other another Jochanan, who was to become, along with one other, Judah, the man from Kiriot, Yeshua's closest and most beloved disciples.

Then *my* Jochanan hastened away to continue his calling of the people. "I urge them to repent," he told us, "to turn around in the deepest seat of their consciousness and prepare to listen to a new messenger from the Whole on High."

By the day of the wedding in Cana, Yeshua had several followers — mostly fishermen. There was Andreas's brother, Simon Peter and a gentle soul called Philippos. Already one or two others hovered round this little circle, clearly interested but not sure how far they were prepared to commit themselves to this new teacher ...

Anyway Jochanan, Andreas, Peter and Philippos all came with us to the wedding and witnessed what happened towards the end of the feast.

They ran out of wine.

And Maryam told Yeshua.

"They have no wine," I heard her say quietly.

He looked astonished. Angry even? No, astonished.

Then he said a strange thing to His mother, such a strange thing.

"Mother, leave me alone. I am not ready ..."

"Yeshua," I heard her say, "if not now, when?"

It was as if they were talking a language known only to them.

Then I saw Maryam turn to the servants and say almost in a whisper, "Do whatever he tells you to do ..."

Yeshua heard her, but said nothing.

In the very midst of the joyful noise of the feast I was aware of silence, deep, deep silence. Even though Yeshua spoke then to the servants the words came out of a great silence, and although he spoke to them calmly it was as if, behind the simple words, there was a coming together of some great force ...

All he said to them was, "Fill the pots with water."

And when they had done so, all he said was, "And now carry them to the master of these ceremonies ..."

The servants poured from the pots into the cups of the guests and everyone began to sip and drink.

The master of the ceremonies leaned towards the bridegroom and said,

"Well, I must say: Most people serve the best wine first, but you have kept it to the last, and it is indeed very good."

The bridegroom looked surprised, embarrassed even and just about managed to smile graciously.

I was standing next to the other Jochanan, who I learned later had studied long with *my* Jochanan and heard him say, as if from now on he would need no convincing of anything Yeshua might do, "Yes! It is true then — he *can* connect with the Whole on High ... He can bring about changes in matter itself ... I *saw* the water; I *saw* Him look upon the water; and when He looked upon the water I *saw* the water turn rose red ..."

Maryam turned to me and just said, "I understand nothing now, but that It has begun."

Once we were home again I continued to wonder at what I had seen at that wedding.

His reluctance to use His powers?

Maryam's strength.

His acceptance to act.

That great silence.

And I saw that none of us were to get off lightly. There was to be no stepping into a garment of magic; a miracle required an immense effort; He and we would all have to go *through* a very narrow, very hard path. Having been born into this world He shared our lower nature; that He would long for the cup to pass from Him to some other ...

And I was frightened — for Him and for my son and those eager disciples. For Maryam and for myself.

Jenny Koralek

PART THREE - V

'These things said he in the synagogue, as he taught in Capernaum. Many therefore of his disciples, when they had heard this, said, This is an hard saying; who can hear it?'

After the wedding Yeshua withdrew alone into a desert place where there were caves for shelter — something He was to do very often for the rest of His days.

We did not immediately move to Bethanehyeh, or Bethany as it was mostly called. I think we were in a state of stupefaction: haunted by what had happened at Cana.

Maryam was very quiet. Often I caught her with her spindle lying idle, while she seemed to gaze into some place where I could not follow; or with her eyes closed, head slightly bent as if listening to a voice I could not hear. More than once I saw her nod, a tiny inclination of the head, once, twice, thrice, but whether in acquiescence or in affirmation of something now understood, how could I possibly know?

No, we did not move at once but, when Yeshua returned from the wilderness we often accompanied him as He continued his way through the countryside with His first disciples.

And that is how it happened that we were present at Capernaum.

That was after the loaves and the fishes, where He had fed a huge crowd with physical food by bringing about an extraordinary 'change in matter' which had made us both weep with a joy we simply could not understand.

After teaching His many, many followers for three days, He took us and the disciples up the mountainside and away from the flatter grassland by the lake.

We had been meditating with Him. He often called us to this — drew us away from the crowds into silence. It was a vibrant silence such as Maryam and I had often practised at Bethanehyeh, and which, because of His immense presence took on a depth and produced a nourishment far beyond anything we had ever known.

And it is of nourishment I now speak.

We became aware of more and more noise and murmurings far below us. And then we heard Him say, "Philippos, look at them all! Even after three days they will not leave and go home. There must be several thousand of them. They must be hungry."

He stood up and said, "We must go down to them," and as we followed Him down to the crowd He called out to them, "Sit down! Sit down and rest!" and then, softly, to Philippos: *Whence shall we buy bread, that these might eat?*

Andreas pointed to a boy nearby. "He's got a few barley loaves and a couple of little cooked fish in his basket. *But what are they among so many?*"

Yeshua beckoned to the boy and with a smile said, "Will you give me your bread and your fish?"

The boy, dazzled by the radiant goodness emanating from Yeshua, came forward, holding out his basket.

"Yes, sir, yes," he said.

And we saw Yeshua bless the bread and the fish with the ritual blessing before food, and then begin with swift and nimble fingers to break up the bread and the fish into little pieces and start handing them out.

The bread never ran out and neither did the fish.

Soon the disciples were asking for baskets or anything to fill with the food and pass through the crowd, and still the food did not run out. There was enough for everyone. Indeed, there was enough to fill a dozen baskets.

Contented now, the crowds broke up and drifted away.

I turned to Maryam, and this time we shared those tiny nods. I knew for myself that they were both indeed an acquiescence and an affirmation of something far beyond ordinary understanding.

'And the Word was made flesh and dwelt among us …'

Yes, that feeding was just before Capernaum where he stood in the synagogue and told us that <u>He</u> was <u>food</u> …

Among that great crowd there were men and women who could not bear to go home. They lingered on the shore, hoping perhaps for at least a glimpse of Yeshua, but once more He slipped away by Himself. He must have known by then that His extraordinary actions must have reached the ears of His enemies; that soon now the authorities would try to arrest Him for causing all these public disturbances.

So He slipped away alone while we took a boat from Tiberias and set out towards Capernaum.

Suddenly one of the Lake's famous squalls blew up out of nowhere. Truly it was a fierce and frightening storm, which hit the boat sideways even though we were really never very far from the shelter of the shore. Silently we were all afraid as we all knew of many sudden sinkings in such storms.

Then, as the men struggled with the oars with all the skills they had learned from years of fishing in those waters — we saw Him. He was walking towards us — walking — I was going to say it seemed, but no, I must tell the truth: He was walking on the water. And no, although we were quite close to the shore, the water there was far from shallow. He walking <u>on</u> the water as if lifted by the very breaths contained in the Holy Four Letters, YHVH (yod, hey, vav, hey).

I will never forget the impressions I received on that boat, in that storm, the darkness of the sky, of this man – man? — steadily coming towards us, lightly, barely, treading the choppy waves as if He were walking on the high road to Jerusalem.

As He came ever nearer we heard Him call out: "Don't be afraid! It is I …"

The moment He laid his hand on the side of the boat the storm ceased. The moment He sat down among us time itself ceased, and we found ourselves immediately at Capernaum.

I am sure that the turmoil, the puzzlement, the awe which battled within me was shared by all the others. Only Maryam, I saw, was tranquil. Long after I had seen with my own eyes the fact, the truth of Him — that unlike us He was not dependent solely on the physical body — I realised we had witnessed laws of another and more subtle level manifesting in our world, witnessed in other words, <u>miracles</u>.

All were silent as we climbed out of the boat; there were none of the usual gasps of relief at the storm being over; no questions expressed out loud about the mysterious actions of Yeshua.

No. Silence, very private silence: no catching of another's eye; no sharing of raised eyebrows. Silence as we all began a further absorption of what was happening more and more often — inexplicably, immeasurably mysterious, in front of which words seemed futile.

Next day the crowd, the faithful crowd had made their way from Tiberias and it was not long before He was once more surrounded and followed into the little synagogue.

"When did you get here? You weren't in the boat with your friends when it set off."

Yeshua did not answer the questions directly. He just said, "Truth to tell, you didn't come looking for me because of the signs. You came looking for me because of the food — food for your hungry bellies. But don't work for that food alone — that kind of food soon goes bad. No, there is another kind of food to work for ... the kind which feeds another part of you — the part that belongs to your search for God ... That is another kind of hunger ... it is a kind of longing ..."

"You say we weren't interested in your signs," said someone. "Well, show us one now while our bellies are full ..."

"Yes," cried another "What can you do that Moses couldn't? He found manna from heaven in the desert and fed the children of Israel ... So what can you do different? What can you do more than that?"

Yeshua — how can I begin to describe — how Yeshua was at that moment ... ?

He seemed to grow large — in the same way that I had sometimes seen Hannah, Maryam's mother, grow large. It was as if He had taken on a stature belonging to something more than an ordinary human being ... as if he was <u>filling</u>, filling with a great presence, a great force.

Then very quietly, very firmly he said, "I am the food — no, not I, but the I AM which dwells in me. The I AM which puts the flesh of words onto Being ... Feed on this I AM, feed on me, so that this Being can dwell within you as the very presence of the Whole on High ..."

You could hear the shock in the fidgeting silence which followed these words.

And then one small voice was heard saying, "Sir ... Lord ... always help us to this food ..."

But altogether the crowd seemed to be shrinking, falling back and we saw people near the doors leaving. A gap appeared in the throng and I suddenly noticed three rabbis sitting in the dark interior of the synagogue. One of them now stood up and said, "How can you dare to say this? Aren't you the son of Joseph of Nazareth, the master carpenter? Why, we all knew him and his parents ..."

Yeshua said sternly yet courteously, "Did you really hear what I said? You most surely know and believe the sacred teachings of the past, the words of the prophet Isaiah, *they shall all be taught by God?*

"Do you really hear what I am saying? That this food of I AM comes directly down from on High — comes through me but is not of me, is not mine. As I said, I AM is this living food of presence which cannot die when the body dies. This food is now in my flesh, in my blood. Feed on me — not I, but the I AM that dwells in me. Feed on me. Feed on me and you too will be fed with that which cannot die when the body dies ..."

I saw from the rabbis' faces that they had shut to Yeshua's words, shut themselves completely and stood up now, stony cold, and then they walked out, looking neither to left or right. They walked out and they were far from the only ones. Many in the crowd followed fast on their heels, and then a fair number of Yeshua's own followers moved away — men and women who, up till now, had been with him always and everywhere he taught — many of them slowly, sadly as if torn in two.

"No," I heard one say. "That is too much ..." "Yes," another agreed. "He's gone too far ... It's too hard, too difficult, the effort He is demanding ..." "Could not ..."

I caught these fragments, and before long the circle around Yeshua had indeed thinned.

But one rabbi, Nicodemus, who I had quite often seen lingering on the edge, was still there. We women were there. The twelve he had not long chosen were there: Simon, Andreas, his brother; Jochanan and Jacob, also brothers, Thomas Didymus, Bart Almai, Thaddeus, Matthias

Levi, Simon Zelotes, that gentle Philippos, the other Jacob, son of Alphaeus and yes, that tragic, great one, Judah Ish Kariot ...

Yeshua looked at us all, and now I know that is the exact moment when I sensed the beginning of a sadness which would never be far from Him for the rest of His days.

"Are you going to leave me too?" He asked.

Maryam laid her small hand on His, lifted it to her lips and kissed it.

Simon, impetuous Simon, fell to his knees while all the others moved closer and closer to this great teacher.

"No!" said Simon. "No, we will <u>never</u> leave you!"

And, "No, No", all the rest of us joined him, murmuring with full hearts, "No, no. Never!"

Capernaum, Capernaum — "the place of hard sayings" as it came to be known. Capernaum was terrifying, for it was there in that synagogue that He threw down the challenge, the challenge which lay behind everything He ever said or did. A moment of truth, a moment of choice from which many turned away never to return.

PART THREE - VI

'The Essenes wished to attain the goal of the prophets through a simplification of the forms of life, and from them was born that circle of men that supported the great Nazarene and created his legend, the greatest triumph of myth.' (Martin Buber)

'If I forget thee, O Jerusalem: let my right hand forget her cunning. If I do not remember thee, let my tongue cleave to the roof of my mouth.' (Psalm 137)

It was not long after that Maryam and I left Nazareth and moved down to Bethany, to that other house of I AM, one of the rays shining out from Jerusalem. I mean, of course, the Jerusalem of the heart, the centre, which if and when it does not hold, is not held by us, brings about all forms of disintegration. The Jerusalem which the Psalm tells us we forget at our peril.

Outwardly this Bethan-ehyeh was the small town of Bethany, and the house a modest one, the home of Yeshua's beloved friends, Eleazer, Martha and Maryam, another Maryam.

There was, long ago, another Eleazer, the servant of Abraham (if servant is the right term) — totally trusted, loved, depended upon, who practised that real, selfless giving we call devotion. I soon saw that this Eleazer stood in this kind of relation to Yeshua.

Martha was the elder of the sisters, always busy, attentive within and without, with that special beauty of a plain woman upon whom life has worked its sorrow and joy.

As for Maryam, she was pretty with her long, long hair which tended to come loose and curl around her headscarf however hard she tried to keep it tidy. Her lovely eyes rested almost all the time on Yeshua with hunger — not of ordinary body desire but of longing for more of Him, of His presence and His words.

The beloved mother of our teacher and I were warmly welcomed. The little house they had found for us across the courtyard was ready for us, and had been thoughtfully prepared for us — as if Martha already knew the simple things that would make us comfortable.

Somehow, I felt, the pot of bright flowers from the fields had not been her handiwork — perhaps that of her dreamy sister, but in that I was mistaken.

There was another Maryam, and it was she who had picked the flowers.

No longer young, gaunt, her face lined with past tensions, she was still a very beautiful woman. She came from the village of Magdala, yet by her bearing and the way she dressed — in richly woven stuffs, and always wearing a small amount of gold; with her long, thick, auburn hair kept back from her face by jewelled combs, or a veil — she gave the air of a worldly woman.

Apparently, however, she had belonged to Yeshua's circle almost from the moment He made Bethanehyeh His home.

A woman long since dissatisfied with her life, long seeking guidance to its meaning, she had been at Capernaum. Undaunted by Yeshua's harsh sayings, she had stayed, made friends with Martha and her sister and, not long after, met Yeshua.

During our meetings with Him she always sat at the back of the room with Martha.

Often I saw that her eyes were full of tears.

"Why is she so sad?" I finally found the courage to ask Martha. "She weeps with joy at a sense of homecoming. She weeps with joy because she is in love with Him ... and He with her."

Oh, how I was shocked!

This was a world far from mine and about which I knew nothing.

Martha had spoken in such a way that she clearly did not invite a response or a visible reaction.

I said nothing, but as the weeks went by I became more and more aware of the look which passed often between Yeshua and Maryam of Magdala.

It was as if in that gaze a world of understanding was passing between them.

And indeed, Maryam and I lived to witness the place Maryam was to take among us all, and then I remembered what I had seen, and felt humbled by my shallow grasp of human relationships.

And when I said so to <u>my</u> Maryam she smiled, and when she answered her voice was very tender.

"He only said something about it to me once, and it was this: 'I love Maryam. We understand one another,' and we have lived to see what he meant."

Jenny Koralek

PART THREE - VII

'Ecstasy (hitlahavut) is embracing God beyond time and space.

'... a man can say "Enough!" to the multiplicity within him. When he collects himself and becomes one, he draws near to the oneness of God — he serves his Lord. This is service (avoda).'

'Intention (kavana) is the mystery of a soul directed to a goal. Not only to wait, not only to watch for the Coming One: man can work toward the redemption of the world. Just that is intention: the mystery of the soul that is directed to redeem the world.'

'... the individual is not a whole, but a part and so much more actively there stirs in him the community of existence. That is the mystery of humility (shiflut). "If Messiah should come today," a zaddik said, and say, 'You are better than the others,' then I would say to him, 'You are not Messiah.'"
(Martin Buber in *The Legend of the Baal-Shem*)

And now began the first period of many of our secret meetings with Yeshua, where we received the most intensive, inspiring and demanding teachings far beyond anything any of us had so far experienced. For of course he did not spend all the time on the road preaching. I think that these times of working with us were as necessary for Him as they became for us.

Four things he taught us first — the same four things we had been taught, Maryam and I long ago in that place of preparation. He taught them, perhaps, in order to be sure of the foundation for what came later — towards the end.

The four things began in the only place they could begin — with the inspiration and experience in His presence of ecstasy — a proper kind of ecstasy, the kind which flings oneself outside oneself, which casts off the little self.

Maryam His mother was His great help in all this, for she had long moved to a place in herself where that little self no longer exerted any force. And her ecstasy was pure, contained, yet glowing.

The rest of us were inspired by them both. Our souls caught fire from theirs.

And if Maryam's ecstasy glowed, His very body seemed aflame, a bright light emanated from Him from just above His head, spreading out around His body, almond-shaped right down to His feet, which shone where He firmly stood on the earth itself.

Ecstasy, He told us, is the first necessity, but not the ecstasy which sends one flying upwards to the far heights of bliss. No — for that distances us much too much from the earth where we live and move and have our being. Indeed, he told us, our dancing, where feet return again and again to the ground itself, expresses in the very body the rapture of ecstasy. Furthermore — once one has fallen in love with the inner YHVH it has to be nurtured step by step, as if one were climbing a long ladder, by a very steady, faithful, regular work — prayer of the kind He and my son had learned in their special community as we had learned it in ours. It cannot be left to an occasional, passionate whim in the uncertain, capricious activity of our hearts. No, it can only set us on fire if we have prayed daily and often, praying *for its own sake with no thought for the fruits of the action*, without any wish for reward or result.

Indeed, when Yeshua saw that our souls were on fire, He grew stern and showed a rigour — a tender rigour — we had not seen before.

"On its own", He told us, "it is not enough. It has a great energy. I can see that you all feel it and that you do not know what to 'do' with it ... but if this energy is not put to good use what will happen to it? It could trickle away like water into earth, or it could drive a man, or a woman, to a kind of madness — a madness of dreams, fantasy, imagination of great, lofty states of bliss which on their own lead to nowhere, to nothing. No, this ecstasy, the energy of this rapture, this love, must be poured into service, into the love of others, our neighbours and the stranger on the road or at the door. And, if the love is right the neighbour, the stranger will sense that it emanates from the Whole on High and they too will be touched, warmed by the fire which comes from this ecstasy, this rapture."

And then He would speak to us of service, of <u>giving</u>.

"Before we can give to, or serve another," He would often say, "we must become 'one' in ourselves. Each human being has a spark of the Whole on High within, which needs help to break out of the hard shell which surrounds it ... From our ecstasy comes the energy to bring a life force, subtle and beneficent to the community in which we find ourselves.

"Every day should be a Sabbath.

"When we collect ourselves we draw near to the Whole on High ... We are serving the Whole on High.

"No special act is asked of us, but all our acts from the humblest to the highest can serve to serve.

"The spark in each human being is the spark of the Shekinah, the manifest, indwelling part of the whole, seeking to be re-united with the unmanifest, hidden Whole on High.

"Each time we try to collect ourselves and each time, not just and only in the silence and privacy of our innermost chamber of prayer, but also out there in the market place, the fields, in our fishing boats, when bringing fire, water and flour together for the baking of bread, when washing clothes at the river bank, drawing water from the well, spinning thread, carding wool, shearing sheep, collecting ripe figs from the fig tree or harvesting the sweet ripe grapes, walking to the next village, tending a sick child or grandfather, tethering our donkey, burying the dead, giving birth, loving a husband or a wife, planing wood, lying down to sleep; waking at sunrise — that moment between sleeping and waking which marries the two worlds. Each time we collect ourselves while in action we know the Kingdom of Heaven. We know it in this possibility of making holy each act. We know it when we are joined with that great energy of rapture, that fine vibration which pours down from above."

This is how he spoke to us often and then He would dance with us and we all entered into that, Maryam and I as joyfully as when we had danced with Eva, Sarah and the other women, long ago ... and the contact of hand in hand, hand on shoulder, arms linked brought us all ever closer.

After these meetings Maryam and I would talk quietly about what He had said.

"This is His work," Maryam always insisted. "To redeem the world, to raise up the sparks and free them from the hard encrustations which make their prison. This is His work with those called blind, deaf, mute or lame, or invaded by devils. He lets the rays in so that they can see, hear, speak, limp no more, be at peace in their clean-swept bodies, hearts and minds. And, even more important, Elizabeth, we have both been there when through His very presence and the words that come out of Him from that presence, a man, a woman suddenly sees, hears, experiences this new way of understanding; sees new sights, hears new sounds. And haven't you noticed when finally they leave, having lingered, reluctant to part from Him, how they walk away upright, with a more spacious breadth to them, a steady gait and head held high?"

Sometimes she would sigh and say, "Yet I fear that these will be recounted as the signs and wonders of a miracle worker who has restored bodily ills, not interior ones ..."

"But," I reminded her each time, "He does also heal the sick ..."

"Indeed, yes," she always agreed, "He has the energies within Him to bring about all kinds of healing, but His work is this raising of the sparks. And we are privileged to witness how the manner of each raising is unique to the individual. We are seeing each time how He breaks down that hard outer shell so that the spark may free itself ..."

Once she fell silent for a long while and then said, "I'm thinking of that woman ..."

"The adulteress?" I asked.

Only a few days before this conversation we had been present when a woman accused of adultery had been brought before Yeshua by a group of men we had often seen praying very loudly in the synagogue. We had stood at the back of the crowd, the only women there, trembling for her, waiting for the stoning to begin. In fact we had been about to turn on our heels and creep away.

"Yes ... and how what He did was not just for her. He knew those men had at least a grain of conscience. He knew it would stir them when He said to them, 'Let the one who has never sinned throw the first stone' ..."

"And he was right — they all shuffled away, shamefaced, stricken ... But what was he doing, writing in the earth with that stick?"

"Avoiding their eyes," said Maryam. "Wanting them to act sincerely, from themselves, from the heart, without the beam of His eye piercing them; wanting them to be touched of their own accord by His few quiet words, to acknowledge that they were no freer from fault than she ..."

"I nearly wept," I said, "when at last He <u>did</u> look up and said to her, 'You see, they did not, after all, judge you, and neither do I, so go now and sin no more ...'

"And she will not, for I heard my son murmur to her, 'Can you be faithful to this new taste of freedom in the depths of your being? Faithlessness to that would be another kind of adultery ...'; and she nodded."

"She was weeping as she left, but perhaps as much in joy as sorrow ..."

Jenny Koralek

PART THREE - VIII

'So that this deification and transformation of earth into heaven can come about, complete and absolute overturning and upsetting of our being is necessary. This change, this upsetting, is called rebirth. The rebirth is threefold: firstly, the rebirth of our reason. Secondly, the rebirth of our heart or will. And finally, the rebirth of our whole being.

The first and second are <u>spiritual rebirths</u>; and the third, <u>corporeal rebirth</u>. Many serious men in their search for God have been reborn in the mind and will, but few have known this rebirth of the body.'
(Karl von Eckhartshausen in *The Cloud Upon the Sanctuary*)

And then there was the matter of Eleazer — Eleazer (spoken of as Lazarus in the Roman tongue), the most faithful and devoted servant of Yeshua, not one of the twelve who became His committed disciples, chosen by Him, but one who already had his special place, who had himself chosen to serve Yeshua while working beside Him all those long years in that special community from which he, like Yeshua and my son, had not long returned. Eleazer's place was unique to him in the heart of our teacher.

He died, you see.

Eleazer died.

And Yeshua brought him to life again.

The magnitude of this event matches the value which Yeshua set upon the family who lived in that house in Bethany — Eleazer and his sisters, Martha and Maryam.

Certainly this was no ordinary family; no ordinary house, but the very centre and heart, the hearth itself of Yeshua's work.

"I think that Eleazer did not need to be a follower in the manner of the twelve," Maryam said to me later. "No, he understood by intuition, as a good servant does, what was needed. He understood and practised my son's counsel to die, to awake, to be born, born afresh, not from the womb, but from the heart and through the spirit, through the constant breathing in and breathing out of **Yod, Hay, Vav, Hay**..."

Eleazer's sisters were remarkable too, and also had special places not only in Yeshua's heart, but in the roles they played, which taught those around them that there might be necessary stages and degrees of possibility in bringing His teaching alive and right into daily life.

Martha was the elder of the two girls — not pretty like her sister, Maryam. Not pretty, but with a certain piquancy to her plainness — a pointed nose to match her sharp tongue, large brown eyes, kind, watchful; a capable work-worn body, and rough-skinned hands; always busy about the house, it seemed she was the one who cooked, baked, swept and cleaned.

I never caught her sitting down, except that is when Yeshua was teaching, and even then she always sat at the back, near the door, ready to jump up and slip out to see to the meal.

Maryam, on the other hand, was a dreamy girl — lovely face, beautiful untidy hair. Unlike her sister she always sat right at Yeshua's feet, cross-legged, leaning on an elbow, or kneeling back on her heels, hands placed on her knees, trying to relax in the way he told us to.

Their way with Yeshua — all three of them — was of the greatest courtesy, yet free and easy with that intimacy which goes with deep, reciprocal, loving friendship, as if this family were close kin to him, brother and sisters even. As Maryam once said, "I feel as if this is Yeshua's real family, the family He did not have ..."

I was touched by Maryam's intensity, sitting there day after day, drinking in Yeshua's every word and faintly irritated by Martha's activity, which seemed to me distracted attention. She often stood in the doorway, one ear on the teaching, the other on the pan bubbling on the fire. I said so one day to *my* Maryam and was astonished and humbled when she said quite sternly, "No, Elizabeth, no, you are not seeing true, hearing right. Watch her without judging. Watch her freshly."

A few days later I heard Martha complaining to Yeshua.

"It's all very well," she was saying, "my sister sitting there, always at your feet like a sweet puppy dog, listening to your every word while I have to attend to everything ... and you ... you never *say* anything to her!"

"Martha, Martha!" I heard Him say, "have you forgotten that you once did as now your sister does? It is a necessary stage if she is to know the one needful thing — the Whole. You too once could only sit and do nothing more than listen, but for a long time now you have been able to go about your tasks without losing touch with your interior world of quiet and stillness. Your sister is not yet able to achieve the two at once, but I know, most surely, that that is what you wish for her — that she too should become a fiery spirit as you now are, your two natures joined in the service of the Whole. Martha, dear Martha, continue your way of doing and being and allow your sister to be, so that in time she too shall be as blest as you are ..."

I saw Martha wipe away a tear and roughly seize Yeshua's hand and kiss it. She seemed about to speak, but before she could, He smiled at her and said, "No, Martha, no guilt, no shame." Then he lifted her red chapped hand to his lips and held it there for some long while.

I could not help but tell Maryam what I had overheard. She said, "Have you noticed — whenever He says a name twice, or repeats His words, Truly, Truly, you know without doubt that this is a moment of great importance for the one He names twice, for those who are listening to Him at that moment?"

Jenny Koralek

PART THREE - IX

'A miracle can only be a manifestation of laws which are unknown to men or rarely met with. A 'miracle' is the manifestation in this world of the laws of another world.'

(P D Ouspensky, quoting G I Gurdjieff in *In Search of the Miraculous: Fragments of an Unknown Teaching*)

There we were then, my Maryam and I, part of the intimacy and intensity which was that family, was that house.

Even so, nothing had prepared me for what happened with Eleazer.

But, if there was to be the most sober manifestation imaginable of the true meaning of Yeshua's teaching, of the reason for his birth; the justification for the labours of His mother in preparing herself for His advent — the second birth, the second awakening, which can only come after a certain kind of dying, where else but within a heart, a mind, a body of the utmost devotion and faith, within safe, known walls, surrounded by trust and love?

He was not there, Yeshua, when Eleazer fell ill with a great fever, shaking and shivering, unable to eat, barely able to sip even a drop of water, so that Martha was reduced to moistening his lips as frequently as she did his brow.

Dry-eyed, red-eyed, after two sleepless nights Martha told us in a whisper that she had sent a message to Yeshua. "I feel in my bones that He best come quickly if He wishes to see my brother alive ..."

At dawn on the third day of his illness, dozing one on each side of his bed Maryam and Martha came to and saw that their brother was dead.

Weeping they came. "Too late," sobbed Martha, "our master will come too late."

To my surprise it was her sister who, putting her arm around Martha, said quietly, "Whatever time He comes it will be the right time."

Yeshua came the next day. Eleazer had already been wrapped in his shroud, laid in a tomb with the stone hard up against the entrance.

We were sitting with Martha and Maryam, receiving mourners and their sympathies when word came that Yeshua was not far off.

Up jumped Martha and ran to meet Him.

Maryam, however, stayed where she was, silent, composed, and suddenly she seemed grown up.

My Maryam stayed by her, but I slipped out quietly and followed after Martha. I caught up with her just as she found Yeshua.

He was not alone — all the twelve were with Him, Thomas at His side.

"If you had come sooner," Martha said with an abrupt, almost rude, reproach, "perhaps you could have saved him ..."

"No, my dear Martha," came the astonishing reply. "Had I come sooner your brother would have died altogether. He needed those three days to complete his passage ..."

"What are you talking about?" Martha cried out almost angrily in her grief.

Yeshua said nothing, but walked on, and so she turned to Thomas.

"What is He talking about? What does He mean?"

Thomas did not answer at once. He seemed hesitant, whether because he too was mystified, or whether because he felt it was not his place to explain our teacher's words, I was not at first sure, but by his almost reluctant response to Martha's questions, I felt he was in his own awkward way trying to convey something of the meaning ...

"Well," he began, "first He said to us, 'Eleazer has fallen asleep and I must go and waken him,' and when we asked 'Why? Surely he will wake up of his own accord?' He said, 'No, he is dead and I must go to raise him up, but the time is not yet. He has first to pass through something on his own which takes a certain time, a time of darkness like Jonah's in the belly of the whale, a time to see and understand what he is not, to shed the little selves as a tree sheds itself of leaves, to return to the emptiness he was when he was not, which is true fasting; a time to know once and for all that I AM is not the body' ... He told us that we must not — He must not, could not — not even He — interfere with this process ... Then he sighed a heavy sigh and said, 'But also it is good for you that I was not there, for now you will be tried as to the strength of your faith and so will I.'"

"I don't understand," Martha said again.

"I don't understand, dear Martha," said Thomas, "and yet I feel that He did not mean an ordinary kind of dead, and all I knew and I know it still, is that at this moment, now, at His side, when my unbelief is quiet, I too want to trust what He says and experience that kind of sleep, that kind of death ..."

I had to stop for a moment, overwhelmed, uncomprehending, almost afraid, but Yeshua now turned to me and asked me to guide Him to the tomb.

As we passed the door of the house, Maryam came running out followed by all the visitors.

She fell to her knees at His feet, weeping.

"Oh Yeshua!" she cried out. "If you had been here ..."

He interrupted her saying, "Maryam, Maryam your brother will rise again ..."

"I know that!" she said sharply. "I know that on the last day as we have been taught from the cradle he will rise again."

Yeshua bent down and helped her to her feet. Then He covered His face with His hands. He was shaking and let out a groan of pain, but it did not sound like the pain of the body ...

Then, taking Maryam's hands in His again, He said in a low intense voice, which I doubt was heard by any of the crowd, who were restless and murmuring among themselves, "Maryam Maryam, I AM is the resurrection ... Your brother knew this, knows this. Now lead me to the tomb ..."

She obeyed, and when we were all arrived there Yeshua was standing there, very still, staring at the tomb and the stone.

Pale of face, eyes closed, He again let out a groan, and bowed His head briefly.

Then, looking up, He opened His eyes and I saw what I had seen in the past: I saw Him seem to grow in height and breadth and to <u>fill</u>, and the filling produced light in Him, coming from Him and yet at the same time into Him from elsewhere.

"Move the stone!" he then commanded in a strong, but low voice.

"But, Master!" cried Martha. "Think! He has been dead now these four days! He will stink! He will look — he will not look himself any more!"

"Martha, Martha!" said Yeshua with great sadness. "How often have you heard me say in your house that you need a new kind of trust?"

And he turned to some of the men standing there and said again, "Move the stone!" And again came the low moan.

Then he looked upwards and said, "You see, Abba, our father, they need to hear me call upon you and they need to <u>see</u> before they can trust this new kind of trust ... So, I pray for help; I pray for help which I know is most surely there ..."

He stood now close to the opening of the tomb and called out in a loud voice, "Eleazer, arise and come forth!"

And Eleazer suddenly was there, and the smell coming from him was sweet and his face illumined, the same good face, full of love, but illumined. He seemed about to speak, but Yeshua put a finger on his lips and shook His head. Holding out his arms He embraced Eleazer and began to unwind the bindings of the shroud. He was trembling.

Suddenly I understood something of the force He must have called upon. Suddenly remembered how at times when the crowd pressed hard around Him He always seemed to know if someone had touched Him, once even asked, "Who touched me? I feel the energy going out of me."

He stopped abruptly the unwinding, and said to the sisters, standing there frozen in their shock, "Help him and then take him home. I will come soon." Then He turned away and we saw that He was weeping, weeping silently.

He went straight to His mother.

She took Him in her arms and bent over Him, cradling the back of His head, and murmuring mother words as if He were a child again. With the hem of her veil she wiped his cheeks, took His hands in hers and kissed His palms.

He whispered something to her and then walked away from us all.

Everyone understood not to go after Him.

Quickly Simon and the others asked the crowd to leave, and had no difficulty in doing so. They were struck dumb, some looked fearful, some moved beyond tears ...

"Come, Elizabeth," said my Maryam. "Let us too go home and draw upon all we were taught and pray for Him, pray for my son, if I still dare call Him so ...'

At that moment I saw humility incarnate.

*****

We were not there when Yeshua returned to the house in Bethanehyeh, but what we saw of Eleazer in the ever-growing turbulent and fear-filled days that followed was a quiet composure — not a perfected man, not a sudden saint, as if his little person had diminished even more, as if he now knew for certain — and far more than the others — that the struggle for the awakened state to prevail was always <u>the only thing that mattered</u>. His attentiveness and vigilance were now serving Yeshua's inner world, inner needs and would never fail Him.

*****

Later during the days of wonderment after this raising of the dead, Maryam looked up at me from the spindle in her lap and said, "Prayer and fasting; prayer and fasting, it is the all ..."

And I thought she was remembering how Yeshua had told the grateful father of a lad He had healed of his many crazed, sick selves, that with prayer and fasting anyone could do what He had done ...

"That is what my son was doing during those days He did not hurry to Eleazer's side. But what kind of prayer? What kind of fasting? It is not the begging prayer, not the hoping prayer; no, it is much harder than that. It is what we were taught, isn't it, Elizabeth ... It is that opening into consciousness, precarious, risky, because it may not be enough ... And the fasting, it has nothing to do with foregoing food for the physical body.

No, it is the sitting and watching the arisings of what is not one's true self, watching their growth with the threat of being assailed by them and the saying of 'No, that is not I; nor that, nor yet that ...' How many of us can undertake such prayer, such fasting?"

And another time she suddenly said, "They shared something that day, my son and His faithful Eleazer, something which has bound them together forever, and that is why we feel that Eleazer is closer to Him than the others. Eleazer has joined Yeshua in the knowledge of a terrible solitude, an awesome solitude which sits on a knife edge, and which at any moment can fall into a loneliness which can destroy ... Oh, the solitude, the necessary solitude when the deepest consciousness is faced head on by the demon out to seize that consciousness for itself without having laboured for it; or if it cannot possess it, then kill it.

"That sleep of Eleazer's was no ordinary death — that is why Yeshua delayed in coming to him. He knew that Eleazer was striving to eat and not be eaten by his desires, his fears, by all that hinders the awakening to life. He knew because He Himself works on this all the time. It is solitary, hard, awful, but brings also a certain joy."

She ceased speaking, and folded her hands in her lap and a deep quiet fell upon us.

My heart ached for her, because she too knew that same solitude in her every cell, and my heart ached for myself because I did not.

After this I saw how far I was from Maryam and how near she was to her son. She always understood what He was doing. By her presence she sustained Him; by her love energised Him. When He faltered, if He faltered, she did not, not until the very end and even then her lamentation was a silent and accepting one.

PART THREE - X

'He was not that Light, but was sent to bear witness of that Light ... '

I should tell you that the news of my son Jochanan's imprisonment and death came hard and fast after the raising of Eleazer. Word had already reached me some time before that he was teaching in or near Tiberias, the seat of Herod, the tetrarch of Galilee.

I would have wished to cover my ears against the telling of his death but I did not. I knew that I must bear at second hand what he had suffered: first, imprisonment and then, a vengeful death. Imprisonment for reprimanding Herod for having taken up with his brother's wife, Herodias (reproaches which had enraged Herod and the woman).

He must have known that would lead to severe punishment, but who could have foreseen the price of Herod's lasciviousness; calculated the degree of Herodias's savage revenge? A beheading; a beheading which, I was told, Herod did not wish for. Apparently he trembled and demurred, but a promise is a promise, and he had made it in front of his court. He had promised to give his step-daughter, Salome, anything she asked for if only she would dance her sinuous dance of the seven unfolding veils. He could not have known that her mother, Herodias, had commanded her that when the last veil had fallen from her girlish body, she must ask for my son's head.

It was brought to her on a silver dish — my son's head served up on a platter. This image will haunt me even beyond death.

Oh, Jochanan, my son! Jochanan, the man *sent from God*, who considered himself unworthy to undo the straps of his cousin's sandals, and who would *make the way straight for Him*, baptise Him with water and ... die; Jochanan, my son, whose destiny was not to enter the kingdom of heaven, which we others were to learn was not a kingdom at all, not a distant blissful paradise, but a shocking new possibility here and now.

But he had gone to the brink, to the moment before the leap. And if he himself could not make the leap, because of him others would. He most surely understood that he was building the step up to this new understanding? He most surely understood that without the solid ground of the Law there could not be this movement into a new dimension; that you cannot take a step up without the step below. After all, both he and Yeshua had spent many years preparing for these days.

In secret places in the desert, in the mountains, among the oranges and the orange flowers, in the silvery olive groves and by the waters of sometimes tempestuous lakes and sluggish rivers, through the harsh heat of the days, in frost, snow, chill rain, from sunrise until sunset and after, for nearly twenty years they had worked together like their mothers before them, but for far, far longer. They never told us about those years, so I can only imagine from my own experience of preparation, can only imagine that theirs must have been a hundred fold as arduous, as rigorous, as least as uplifting as ours.

Of course he understood.

He knew that he was part of this intended cosmic drama. By the end of the time in those places of preparation we all knew that; all knew our roles, the terrible demands they would make on us: my son never to see the new step, the new bright dimension; another to deny he knew anything about it; another to bear not only his own doubts, but the doubts of Yeshua, His Twin; the women to stand by and watch the pitiless unfolding.

And then there was <u>that</u> one, the most courageous of all, who would be asked to take upon himself a betrayal which will make him most cruelly hated among men until the end of time.

Oh yes, my son, my Jochanan, knew and understood — which does not mean that he did not waver and forget — as did all the others; yes, even her, even the mother, even Maryam.

And where and when did my son first murmur: *I must decrease that He may increase?* Words I was so often to hear him whisper when he thought himself alone?

Jochanan, "the Baptist" and Judah Ish Kiriot. Without those two He would not have been able to carry the action through and to the end and beyond — those two who were prepared to sacrifice, who taught Him the meaning of sacrifice through their own selfless acts, taught Him the degrees of sacrifice, so much that He in His turn knew they would not fail Him, and that He would not therefore fail them, could not fail them, those two great initiates, His teachers, you could say.

"The way must be prepared," perhaps He said to my son beneath the stars, having drawn him away from the others. "I want you to raise your voice for me, for my coming. You are already known. Your voice will be heard. You are listened to, feared even. You already use the language necessary — you know the need for 'repentance': that first turning around, which leads to turning inward and downward into the deepest seat of consciousness. And I have chosen <u>you</u> to do that. You have the strength of those who have lived long in the wilderness. You know the Law and you love it and live it. On that kind of foundation I can build, but your very rigour and honourable righteousness will make it impossible for you to come with me all the way. Will you be able to bear that? Will you be able to endure the consequences, whatever they may be?"

"Although we seemed to be together in all our studies and labours in the place of preparation," Jochanan may have replied, "there came a time when I knew that even if I was almost ready to go out and baptise with water, <u>you</u>, You would be baptising sooner or later not with water, but with ... with a new breathing: Spiritus, Ruach; that You would breathe this new spirit into the very cells and marrow of the men and women who will seek You out, who have been waiting for You without knowing that they were waiting for You ..."

And Yeshua might have continued, "You will have to convince the world that we have not been together in this. You will have to foretell me. And when I appear to you, you will have to say that you did not know me. In this way it will be seen that I am bringing something new ..."

And we know that my son agreed to this: he called himself *the friend of the bridegroom*. He told his own disciples that *the one who comes from above is above all*, and *the one who is of the earth is earthy and speaks of the earth*. Some of his own followers were Yeshua's first disciples. Jochanan stood back. He let them go.

He became a consummate actor. By the river Jordan, when he saw Yeshua coming towards him, what did he say to the crowd around him? *You see, I did not know Him. I just did what he who sent me told me to do.* And they would have assumed he was obeying the commands of the elders of his Community. *I was told to baptise the one over whose head a dove fluttered, and so, when I saw the dove descending ...* And no, he never told anyone who had sent him. It was to be much later, much later, that the other Jochanan, the divine, wrote things down, and said simply that my son was *a man sent from God*, thereby setting a seal on the high calling of my son.

But I still fret over that strange message he sent to Yeshua from the prison, asking if He really was the One. What had happened to ask Him that, when so often I heard him out of his devotion to Yeshua murmuring that phrase, *I must decrease that He may increase?*

Whatever the reason, how understandable that he wavered; was, in that prison, uncertain. Which of us, in the struggle to spiral upwards in our understanding, never slides back down to the more comfortable, familiar known? And even more likely when the stakes are so high? The spiral leading to no less than a leap into a colossal, unknown proposal — no, more than a proposal: a demand — not only to love one's neighbour as oneself, but now also to love one's enemy!

Yeshua gave my son the answer he would understand, but I am told His voice was weary: "Tell Jochanan," he said, "the blind can see, the lame can walk, the deaf can hear and the dead are raised up ..." He knew that this was what my son would want to hear, but whether Jochanan understood <u>and was glad</u> that Yeshua was speaking of a different kind of seeing, walking, hearing and coming back to life — <u>that</u> we were never to know.

My deepest thought leads me to wonder — even believe — that the extent of my son's sacrifice might have included acceptance of not understanding what his once pupil, now teacher, was about.

In my deepest thought I feel awed by my son's act of offering himself to the end, to the very end: the first to show how difficult it is, and often impossible, to cross from one current to another. He had gone far, far further than anyone alive. I would not diminish my son's qualities, my son's convictions, my son's faith, my son's humility. Yeshua never did. Indeed, just after He sent that message to Jochanan, He turned on the people around Him, yes, the disciples as well as the crowd made up of the curious, and the Pharisees' eavesdroppers, turned on them with an anger which Matthias, the tax collector, told me, seemed barely controlled. "What did you expect? *What did you go out into the wilderness to see?*" He asked in a cold, cutting voice, and when no-one volunteered to speak, He went on, "No, tell me! *What went you out to see? A reed shaken in the wind? But what went you out for to see? A man clothed in soft raiment? No, men in fine clothes do not dwell in the wilderness, but in palaces. No, you went out to see and seek a <u>prophet</u>. Yes, and more than a prophet* — a messenger sent to prepare the path for me, for the new ..."

By this time, Matthias told me, the people were cowering, even trying to step backwards, but He went on, "*But no, it was a <u>prophet</u> you saw ... perhaps Elijah even, come again as was promised. 'A prophet?' I hear you mutter. A prophet? Yes! And more than a prophet ... a messenger ...* sent to prepare and clear the pathways for the very breath of God ... the Word made flesh ... But you took no notice of him. You did not recognise him. You were blind to the magnitude of his task, you did not acknowledge his self-sacrifice ..."

I can believe He was angry. He loved my son, and had looked up to him from childhood, Jochanan, His cousin, older by a few months, who looked after Him if He fell, who played with Him and later taught Him the Law in the Torah, the Psalms, the Prophets' words and prayed with Him.

He was devastated by the news of Jochanan's death. They all came to tell me that. Devastated. Tears filled His eyes. He wiped them away again and again with his fists. He called all the disciples to go with Him away from the crowds into a boat upon the lake, and they crossed into a deserted place, where they sat around Him, appalled by the degree of His sorrow.

Only after a long while did Yeshua look about him and saw again those crowds He had left on the other shore.

And then, Matthias told me, "He closed His eyes and seemed to be listening to an invisible speaker. Then He opened his eyes and said to them, 'It is as if I hear Jochanan's voice saying, 'Continue! Continue! Your work must go on.' He stood up and, pointing, said, 'Look at them! Look at them! They have been there for hours. They have not fled in fear of me. I must go to them. And you must come with me. I cannot fail the one who did so much to prepare the way for me ...'"

And the disciples followed Him back down to the boat and went with Him to the other shore where, His soul on fire, Yeshua began to describe the Kingdom of Heaven in myriad and marvellous ways, likening it to all that was familiar to those farmers and fishermen: As a grain of mustard seed *which indeed is the least of all seeds but when it is grown it is the greatest of herbs and becomes a tree so that the birds of the air come and lodge in its branches.*

As the yeast a woman added to her flour, enough to make all her bread.

As a fishing net *that was cast into the sea and was hauled in, full of good fish which was put to good use ...*

Like a man who discovered treasure in a field and sold everything he possessed so that he could buy that field.

Like a sower who went forth to sow *and some seeds fell by the wayside and the fowls came and devoured them up; some fell on stony ground where they had not much earth and when the sun came up, they were scorched because they had no root, so they withered away; some fell among thorns and the thorns sprung up and choked them. But other seed fell into good ground and brought forth fruit, some an hundredfold, some sixtyfold, some thirtyfold.*

He likened these seeds to the men and women who hear His word about the kingdom of heaven — the ones who receive it on the stony ground within themselves are joyful, but only for a time, for the kingdom cannot take root in them; the thorns are the cares of this world which choke the word, but the man or woman who receives the word with an open heart, that is the good ground of understanding, and bears fruit in quantities according to the degree of that understanding ...

But while Yeshua went on his way, inspired by my son's death to pursue his way ever more passionately I lay for many nights sobbing, huddled with Maryam in the bed. She never reproached, never tried false comfort, but murmured and stroked my hair and smoothed my brow and crooned to me as if I were her little child going and coming in and out of a nightmare.

In my meanest moments I was bitter, so bitter: my son gone; my son dead; Eleazer restored to new life.

I shut myself away and it was some time before I could bear to hear from Maryam, of the honest words Yeshua had for my son, and the precise worth He put on him: *"He was a burning and a shining light. Among those born of women there is not a greater prophet than Jochanan the Baptist."* I took great comfort from those words and simply did not hear, as if I had become deaf overnight, what he also said: *"But he that is least in the kingdom of heaven is greater than Jochanan."*

It was only after Yeshua's own death, and because of everything I had by then witnessed, that I began to understand His teaching more deeply, and was able to open myself to that last statement.

A day came at last, bringing solace and reassurance, when I suddenly remembered how Jochanan had explained in lovely images how he saw his role.

"For one to reach the summit," he had said, "there must be another below him, and another on whose shoulders he stands, and another below him, and another, and another, not one of whom may ever see the rare bird with rainbow feathers at the top of the tree, or touch the moon's cold crescent dipping over the ultimate peak, or be consumed by the fire of the sun itself ..."

At last I was able to acknowledge what my son had so clearly understood – that there are as many levels needed to reach the Whole on High as there must have been rungs on that ladder which Jacob had seen on his dark night.

Jenny Koralek

PART THREE - XI

'Judah, I am only he who sitteth in thy heart. I am faith. I dwell in each heart in that measure in which each heart can hold me.'
(Sholem Asch in *The Nazarene*)

Maryam grew to love all the twelve and showed them equal kindness.

But I could tell that in her heart of hearts there were three who were specially dear to her: Simon, Thomas and ... Judah Ish Kiriot ...

When she first saw Thomas she fainted, and when I was ministering to her she said to me, "That is His holy twin, Thomas Didymus ... I saw him before once long ago when Yeshua was a tiny boy — and he, Thomas, the same height and age, came running and embraced him and ... and ... *disappeared into Him*. Oh, it was a dream! It must have been! And I called him then 'the Twin' the other part of Him, His soul's companion ..."

And later, much later, whenever Thomas expressed his doubts at Yeshua's words and actions, Maryam wept and when I tried to comfort her she said over and over, "He has taken my son's doubt of Himself upon himself ... oh Thomas, courageous Thomas ..." And would turn to me and say, "Is that not love? Is that not love?"

And Simon she loved for his impetuous enthusiasm for her son's teaching, his total faith in Him, his passionate protection of Him, the way he shielded Him from the press of the crowd, was always the first to see when He was exhausted, somehow always ready with his boat to row Him away to a quieter place ... We were both there at that last supper when Simon stood up and declared that never, <u>never</u> would <u>he</u> let him down; never deny knowing Him; there to hear Yeshua's sorrowful reply: *Verily I say unto thee, That this night, before the cock crow, thou shalt deny me thrice ...*

I can still see the sadness on Maryam's face when she heard that Simon had indeed later that same night furiously insisted that he had never been a follower of Yeshua, and had been seen, no sooner were the words out of his mouth, leaning against the wall of the High Priest's house, weeping bitterly.

"Poor man," she said. "He will have at that very moment remembered the words of His teacher ... And only then understood the very great difficulty of His demand, and that Yeshua knows all the dangers, all the pitfalls, knows how strong is our other part, which does not wish for change, for transformation; knows that we must all pass beyond our opposing inclinations, and perhaps Simon more than most, if he is truly to be the strong and steadfast foundation upon which my son hopes to build His new vision of the true meaning of life on this earth ..."

But of the three it was Judah she loved most. Judah, the man from Kiriot.

"He has the hardest role to play," she confided in me once, but when I asked her what she meant she just said, "You will see ..."

In spite of our great intimacy there were parts of Maryam's life where I knew I had no place; no more so, of course, than in her conversations with her son, but also in her relationship with Maryam of Magdala. This was as near, I often thought, as that of a loving mother-in-law and daughter-in-law as could be. Sometimes I wondered if these two Maryams were each a part of the whole form and meaning of the woman He needed to match Him — one a mother, the other a soul-mate, a helpmate, a spiritual equal, a beloved.

It was not long before I felt the privacy of her talks and time spent with Judah.

At first I understood it as part of Maryam's motherly nature, for it was clear from the first day that Judah was an intense, very serious man. In this he reminded me of my son, the once great difference being that his devotion to Yeshua was a silent one. He would sit there hanging on His every word, but never spoke.

So I was not surprised to catch Maryam's tender, protective gaze often resting upon him, always long enough for him to sense it, meet her eye and, having met her eye, relax, soften and smile at her. But if her loving look was intended to encourage him to speak there, even she failed.

However, Judah began to visit her, and whenever he did, which happened more and more often, I would slip away.

Only once did I overhear them, and I feel guilt and shame to this day that I did not move out of earshot.

My excuse still is the terrible state Judah was in when he arrived. Maryam was in the inner courtyard washing lentils and greens when Judah came rushing in, setting the beads of the door curtain into a clatter. He brought his own heated, anguished draught with him, for the man was sobbing, and his eyes so full of tears he was in danger of blundering into our few furnishings.

"Where is she?" he gasped. "Where is the mother? I must see the mother."

I was about to tell him, but she was already there.

"Judah! Judah!" she now said in her quiet but commanding way. "Come now. Come out into our little garden and sit with me, and tell me — what is it? What is it?"

And she led him out among the trumpets of Jericho, the oleander, to our bench beneath the sturdy vine where the grapes were growing darker, fatter by the day …

I saw Maryam sit down.

I saw Judah fling himself at her feet and lay his head in her lap.

I saw her stroking his hair and his heaving shoulders.

I heard his weeping as if his heart was being torn out of him and I was terrified.

I began to turn away to distance myself, so I could not hear him, but then he said, "Oh mother! *I can't! I can't! Now that I have seen Him!* I saw Him! I saw Him!"

Can't what? I thought and then, *What madness. Of course you've seen Him — we all see Him often, nearly every day in fact, so why have you let yourself get into this state?*

"Where?" Maryam asked simply.

"On the mountain. I saw Him on the mountain. I saw Him, yet not Him. I *saw* what He *is*!"

It was then that I gave in to my curiosity and listened.

What did he mean? I asked myself.

But *she* did not ask Judah what he meant.

She seemed to know.

"The others were there," he was saying, "but they fell down in a swoon ..."

"The others?" said Maryam softly. "Simon? Jacob? Jochanan?"

"Yes, yes!" came the reply. "I followed them, you see. I could not help myself. When I heard Yeshua call them aside I knew something momentous was going on — and I could not help it. I *had* to know. I had to be there, but I did not have the courage to ask if I could come too, so I followed them — it was still dark. And so I saw what happened ..."

"What happened?" Maryam asked with her familiar calmness. Nothing concerning Him ever took her by surprise. She wanted to help Judah put into words *his* astonishment — astonishment which had made him speak, of fear, of awe, of conviction of something.

"He ... He ... walked alone to the top of the hill and stood there ... I th ... thought, He's gone up there to pray. Indeed, He did raise His arms upwards ..."

"Did He?" whispered Maryam.

"Yes, He did and ... and ..."

Words were being drawn out of him like thorns deeply embedded in hurting flesh.

"And as He did ... He ... He began to ... *change* ... His form began to change, became transparent. I saw Him in a different kind of body — finer, softer. I knew it was still Him, but radiating now, glowing, suffused with light. Then I saw two others, one on each side of Him ..."

"Elijah. Moses," said Maryam.

"Yes," I heard Judah say, "Elijah. Moses ..."

Now Judah had great being. He had after all been for twenty years with Yeshua and my Jochanan. My son and Yeshua had spoken of him a little when they returned to us, but until we met the disciples who gathered around them, we had never seen him or heard of the bond between them.

In the years Maryam and I shared later, I learned that Yeshua, too, had frequently talked alone with Judah.

You could say that Yeshua had teachers in those two men of great being: Jochanan, my Jochanan, and Judah Ish Kiriot. Who their teachers were we will never know, unless we dare to consider that their instruction came directly from the Whole on High. It would seem certain that many secret things passed between them.

Jochanan and Judah: they each knew the part they would have to play ...

These were the men with the greatest love, devotion, sense of service and above all understanding of the magnitude of Yeshua's teaching: nothing less than bodily rebirth, or birth of a new kind of body before physical death and which would transcend physical death.

Jochanan was to prepare the way for the leap upwards, and Judah to bring about the arrest which would lead to Yeshua's death, resurrection and ascent — Judah who would play for time with the Roman forces so that Yeshua could give His last teachings on love which he, Judah, would not hear; would not hear his final commandment, a new commandment, *That ye love one another; as I have loved you, that ye also love one another.*

No, obeying His teacher, at His almost inaudible words, *That thou doest, do thou quickly*, he quietly slipped away, knowing from that moment on he was to be among the most reviled of men until the end of time ...

What sacrifices these two great men made: neither to live to see the Resurrection and the coming of the Paraclete, that great breath, that great energy, which is the true kingdom of heaven.

Both had been with Yeshua at the feet of the same Master for twenty years. They knew what they had to do. There was to be no escape. Like Yeshua they had been prepared yet still had to suffer very great doubt, very great fear, knowing that only by great struggle, great perseverance would very great faith prevail over all else.

No wonder Judah was in anguish. Having seen Yeshua's full glory, how could he possibly carry out his task?

As I stood there listening to Maryam and Judah, I was horrified, unable to believe my ears. I also felt shame that in spite of all the extraordinary events I had witnessed and taken part in, I still could not accommodate the magnitude of this drama which turned everything completely upside down.

And now I heard him say on a sob, "Oh, mother, how can I? I cannot. I loved Him already, and now seeing the truth of Him, how can I help to bring about His death? I can't ... I can't ... I have <u>seen</u> Him ... Surely if he reveals Himself thus to the world, the world will receive Him?"

Maryam did not say anything and I heard Judah say, "Of course He saw me. Once the vision had faded and while the others slept He came to me and spoke to me. He spoke to me. He said, 'I will need you, your deep, quiet love to help bring about what has to be. I will die, Judah. They will kill me ...' And when I made some noise of protest, He raised His hand to silence me and said, 'But I have to die. I have seen there is no other way. They do not understand. They want it all to be external. They want a king, a reformer, a redeemer from outer oppression. A few have tried to bring about an <u>inner</u> change, but most want something, someone to look at, to look up to, another kind of scapegoat. They don't want to die to themselves here and now in this life, and enter the kingdom I speak of here and now, the kingdom <u>within</u>, which is the possibility of joining with a finer cosmic vibration, allowing the Whole to descend and men and women to ascend, forming a ladder of rays like the one Jacob saw in his dream ...'"

"Obey Him," I heard Maryam say. "Listen to Him. Help Him. Trust Him. It <u>is</u> necessary. I have always known this in my heart — always ..."

Silence.

"Oh mother, dearest mother, I did not mean to make <u>you</u> sad!"

"I am not sad, but I am always sorrowful. I have been sorrowful since the day the angel came and never more so than when I first felt the child leap in my womb, but from that same moment and ever since, joined to the sorrow, I also know a very great joy. Joy is not <u>happiness</u> any more than <u>sadness</u> is sorrow. Through my form, formlessness came into the world — for that is what you saw there on the mountain. You saw my son's secret, my son's dissolution — what He came to teach — the dissolution of assertion of solidity and all the illusion which goes with that ... a melting of selfishness. Love, in fact. Love, indeed ..."

Silence.

"You remember what He said about the grain of wheat? That the seed of new life cannot grow unless it dies in the deep dark earth, worked on by the rain, the sun; worked on until its hard outer casing disintegrates. Only then can it burst forth upwards to the light. Only then can it flower into its true being. And so it must be for Him if He is to show that it can be so for all of us.

"You have been strong till now, knowing your role. Do not fail Him when the time comes. You cannot fail Him, you must not fail Him. He needs you for the fulfilment of His teaching as He needed Jochanan for the birth of it."

Then it was that I came to myself with a certain shame and crept away.

And I saw, before I tiptoed away, I saw them weeping together.

It was not long after Judah and Maryam spoke together that the last great and terrible days began to unfold.

Jenny Koralek

PART THREE - XII

***'If the flesh has become because of the spirit, it is a marvel;
but if the spirit has become because of the body it is a marvel
of marvels.'*** *(The Gospel of Thomas)*

I have never forgotten that day — not long before Passover, when our time with Yeshua, so particularly full of mystery, beauty, goodness and love, started to break asunder; when the restive crowd at the door really began to make itself felt; when Maryam of Magdala made a gesture which was extravagant even for her extravagant nature; and when Yeshua rode to Jerusalem on a lowly donkey.

Why did He do that? Later some said it was His last temptation — that the devil, having failed the first time, returned to entice Him to seize the power and worship due to an earthly king. But Maryam of Magdala denied this passionately and Maryam of Magdala was there ...

Since the return to life of Eleazer there was always a crowd lingering about near the house, sometimes small, sometimes larger, looking to catch a glimpse of him or of Yeshua, hoping perhaps to witness some new amazing 'miracle'.

But on that day their sometimes quite noisy presence outside spread a tension and feeling of disquiet into the house. Well, that is what I felt, but I should put it down to my own inability to remain calm and steadfast. The others seemed able to absorb those emanations.

Of course I should have realised from the intensity of the teachings He had been giving us daily over the past weeks that He was working with us because time was running out. The closer we came to the end — and before we knew that it was not the end — the less I seemed able to understand. The more I saw Maryam's being grow, as she silently pondered on all that was happening, opening to it, evermore surrendering herself, emptying herself, becoming virgin again, the more ordinary I felt myself to be, having to bite my tongue to prevent me speaking from reactions, suffering headaches from straining after insight, sleeping badly, as if expecting to be suddenly awakened and for some appalling demand to be made on me immediately; dizzy from Yeshua's great teachings. Yes, all this should have warned me, but it was only afterwards that I saw He was trying to prepare us for His going, trying to leave us with help, so we would not forget to activate for ourselves His great call to presence; would not forget to nurture the real Self, which comes alive when I can affirm that 'I AM'. "Ehyeh asher ehyeh," "I AM." That is how He began each teaching. And when we were with Him, how could we not experience, however feebly, however fleetingly, these words piercing our flesh, permeating our cells? At such times how far we were from the world and the men who would consider this as blasphemy! And who <u>did</u> consider this as blasphemy and kill Him because of it ...

To this day my heart lightens and my intention deepens when in my solitude I call up Maryam's voice reciting by heart from these teachings, as she so often did in the remaining years we were together: *Verily, verily I say unto you: Before Abraham was, I AM; I AM is the good shepherd ... I AM is the way, I AM is the truth and the life ... I AM is the true vine ... he that abideth in I AM and I AM in him, the same bringeth forth much fruit ... ; the Kingdom of Heaven is in your centres; Let him who seeks, cease not from seeking, for he who seeks shall find, and to him who knocks it shall be opened; If the flesh has become because of the spirit, it is a marvel; but if the spirit has become because of the body it is a marvel of marvels ... ; Become yourselves, passing away ... ; I AM the All: cleave the wood, and I AM there; lift up the stone, and you shall find me there ...* And many other of His sayings she recited, reminding me that everything He spoke of us had to do with the making of an inner world, here and now on this earth ... and that when He spoke of going away it was to prevent us from depending upon Him to do this work for us ... And she would remind me that what He had promised us had come to pass — the sending of the third part of the Whole on High ... the Holy help of the Paraclete, the true Comforter, the Spirit which breathes me, thus keeping alive the contact between above and below.

But all this was yet to come.

That day, then, as we sat down to eat, Maryam of Magdala with one short sharp cry, fell to her knees at Yeshua's feet and began to anoint them lavishly with the healing balm of spikenard from an alabaster jar she was holding. Shocked, embarrassed, puzzled, we watched as she then wiped His feet with her long rich hair.

There was murmuring from among the disciples, many of whom did not like Maryam of Magdala — through jealousy, of course. But before any one of them could voice their disapproval, Yeshua put up a restraining hand and said, "No. Do not speak. Let her be. She has done this in preparation for my death which is soon to come ..."

There was an anguished gasp from all in that room. Some began to weep.

But Yeshua remained exceedingly stern and said, "But now, here we are, now, together, now, companions in the sharing of bread, not only the bread which feeds the body, but the bread I have spoken of which feeds the soul." And he took a piece from the basket and broke it and offered pieces to the disciples sitting on each side of Him. And no-one dared speak a word.

After the meal another strange thing happened. Yeshua called gentle Philippos to Him and asked him to go and find a donkey and bring it to Him.

When Philippos opened the door we could see and hear that the crowd had grown bigger than ever, and an excited shout went up, then died down, disappointed when they saw that it was not Yeshua coming out to them.

But when Philippos returned some while later leading a young donkey a roar of excitement rose up, which only increased when Yeshua came out of the house and mounted the lowly creature.

The disciples crowded round Him, not knowing what He was doing or where He was going.

From the doorway neither Maryam nor I could hear what passed between them, but Maryam of Magdala left her place by the donkey's head and came over to us. "He is going to Jerusalem," she whispered. "I will come and tell you everything that happens, I promise ..."

We watched as the procession set off, the crowd running ahead, some plucking fronds from the palm trees and throwing them down in front of the donkey, some beginning to cry out "Hosanna! Hosanna!"

Just before they passed out of sight we caught a glimpse of another crowd coming towards them and joining with them. We thought we heard the words, *King of the Jews*, but were not sure if we had heard right.

Maryam began to tremble, so I did too. If she was afraid I knew there was good cause.

"This is the beginning," she said. "They will not understand why He is doing this. They will seek in their laws to arrest Him ... and worse ..."

"Wh-why?" I asked. "What will they think He is doing? And what is He doing anyway?"

"He is going to try one more time to remind Jerusalem of Jerusalem ..."

And when I tried to ask her what she meant, she began to turn away indoors saying, "Come, Elizabeth, let us go in and pray for Him ..."

PART THREE - XIII

'And when he was come nearer, he beheld the city and wept over it. O Jerusalem, Jerusalem! ... How often I would have gathered thy children together, even as a hen gathereth her chickens under her wings and ye would not! Behold, your house is left unto you desolate ...'

Maryam of Magdala kept her word, but she did not return for several days.

She was exhausted, dishevelled and desperate.

"Oh the sorrow of it!" she cried, taking Maryam's hands in hers. "The sorrow of it ..."

"Jerusalem did not wish to be reminded of Jerusalem," Maryam said, half affirming, half questioning. "But they did not stop Him from riding into the city?"

"No, and they listened there in front of the Temple against the racket of the bird-sellers and the moneylenders when He cried out, 'O, Jerusalem, Jerusalem, you have forgotten the Zion that dwells in the heart ... *If thou hadst known, thou, at least in this thy day, the things which belong unto thy peace! but now they are hid from thine eyes ...*'"

As I listened to her I began to weep, but my Maryam remained quiet, her hands clasped loosely in her lap. And once more I felt the difference between us. Her ability to contain herself, yet without detaching herself, as if she was able to take upon herself all that was hurled at her, at us all, and to sustain it, and furthermore, able to radiate true calm because she was free of reaction, free of judgement. I felt encircled by her atmosphere and I am sure Maryam of Magdala did too, for she was able to continue with only the slightest tremor in her voice.

"Only those of us standing close to Him, heard Him add: 'Another Babylon. They have brought upon themselves another far more terrible kind of exile ... from their own innermost core ...' And then he dismounted and went into the Temple and began to open the bird cages, which set off an immense fluttering and whirring as the doves flew to freedom in their hundreds, so that the sky grew dark as it does when the swallows leave ... Amid the uproar he strode on, turning over the moneylenders' tables as He went, crying out in a white anger, *'Is it not written, My house shall be called the house of prayer, but ye have made it a den of thieves?'* And I, still pondering on what he had said about the inner Jerusalem, knew that although He was angry at this obscene use of the Temple, the house of prayer is intended to dwell in the heart ..."

She paused and sat back on her knees. "Then he walked out and the crowd, frightened, outraged, speechless, parted to let Him and the disciples through and from there they went to Martha's house.

"But He was back in front of the Temple early next day, and stood there preaching till dusk.

"Many came to listen to Him, among them other rabbis, who kept challenging Him and He answered them every one, and every one of them had to agree that what He was saying was wise and well within the Law. But we also noticed others who were clearly there to report what he was saying to the High Priests. By the second day Simon and the others were very worried that He might be arrested, and finally persuaded Him as the day drew to an end to leave. With his usual skill Simon spirited Him away somewhere down into the lower city, while the rest of us of us went back to Martha's, hoping that those following Him would come to Bethany and not find Him there.

"It worked, and I am here to give you a message — that you should both come with me up to Jerusalem, for Yeshua wishes to celebrate the Passover there and not, as in past years, at Bethanehyeh. He wants us all to be there with Him, for he knows it will be His last. Mother Maryam, you must know it is only a matter of time before He is arrested as a trouble-maker ..."

"I do know," said Maryam, who then stood up and simply asked, "But where will He eat this Passover?"

"In the house of Joseph."

"That good man from Arimathea?"

"That good man from Arimathea. He has offered Yeshua the upper room in his house, and I am to bring you there where there are rooms awaiting you too."

It has not seemed necessary until now to tell you that Yeshua had other followers, beside disciples. Among them this rich and generous and serious man, Joseph, and of course that rabbi, Nicodemon, who would tell us one sad day that he had been about to offer himself and all his own students as disciples of Yeshua, but had left it too late. There was another man too, who had hovered on the edge of our circle for a long time — Simon of Cyrene, a giant of a man, who would also have a role to play.

I left the two Maryams together and went to pack up our few things. When I returned the mother Maryam had refreshed the daughter Maryam with food and water, bathed her, brushed out her lovely hair, taken away her dusty clothes and led her away to bed.

We left for Jerusalem at dawn of that next day.

Jenny Koralek

PART THREE - XIV

'And He took bread and blessed it and said, Take, eat; this is my body.

And He took the cup and gave thanks and gave it to them, saying, Drink ye all of it; for this is my blood ...'

Yeshua was there to welcome us.

It was a shock to see he was wearing His pure white *kittel*, although it should not have been, seeing that is the robe I would have expected Him to be wearing on the eve of Passover, but somehow I had never before noticed how shroud-like the garment was.

"Most beloved mother," He said, taking her in His arms. "How I need you with me at this time."

"My dearest child" she said, kissing Him on each cheek, on each hand.

"And you too, beloved cousin, Elizabeth," He said, drawing me to Him also.

"Thank you, my Maryam, for bringing them to me," He said to the one from Magdala, holding her intense gaze in His.

"Martha is here and her sister, and Eleazer too. All is prepared for our Passover meal, but we waited for you, the two mothers, to light the candles when the first stars appear ... But there is still time for us all to come together and be together in prayer ..."

And He guided us upstairs to the large simple room from where no sound of the outside world reached us, and where the table was all laid with the roasted lamb and its shank-bone, the bitter herbs, the unleavened bread at the centre, the wine, the egg and the *Haroseth* ...

"Martha's *Haroseth*," smiled my Maryam. "I can just see, her pounding all day at her apples and almonds and not allowing her poor sister even to add the cinnamon and raisins ..."

That was the last sweet moment of normality — sometimes I think the last ever ...

For Yeshua then gathered us all around Him at the table. Martha was there and her sister and brother, all the twelve disciples and a place for every one of us.

A silence came down upon us all, and suddenly the room seemed full of a golden light and filled with unseen presences of immense power and benevolence. We were being lifted up, so that even though I am sure, like me, all who were there wanted to bend and bow down under the sense of imminent horror and pain, grief and loss, we all remained upright, relaxed, quiet, tearless.

And while we were in that state and <u>He</u> was in that state, he spoke to us His last teachings, of which now, with my ordinary mind, I can only remember fragments, but the substance, the flavour of which flowed into my cells as it surely did into the cells of all who were there, steeping them in His Being insofar as we were able to absorb It.

"With what desire I have desired to eat this Passover with you before I suffer," He said. *"Heaven and earth shall pass away, but my words shall not pass away."*

"It is fitting," He said, "this being the Night of Watching, that I say to you again, *Watch, for ye know not when the master of the house cometh, at even, or at midnight, or at the cock crowing, or in the morning, lest suddenly he find you sleeping. Therefore, watch ...*"

And He spoke to us one more time of the four needful things for the good: ecstasy, which is love of the Whole on High, service which is love of neighbour, intention which is the orientation towards these two, and humility which is again love of all that lives and breathes.

And many other things He said to us of which I remember only broken phrases, but which I know were written down later by several who were present, and which are read now wherever Yeshua's followers gather.

We prayed with Him. We recited the verse, *Listen, O Israel, the Lord our God IS the all ...*

Then He said, "I know you all try again and again to attune with the Above, and that when you do you are picturing the life and message of the letters which make up these sacred words ..."

And he spoke the letters, one by one: **Shin, Mem, Ayin; Yod, Shin, Resh, Aleph, Lamed; Yod, Hay, Vav, Hay; Aleph, Cheth, Daleth.**

I know before I begin that I can only fail to convey the magnitude of these moments. We were outside time, in another place, another of His Father's *'mansions'* as He once called this other dimension.

Such a stillness came from Him that we were bathed in it.

Then He turned to us, to His mother and to me and said in His usual tender yet commanding way, "Now light the candles for us! For the Passover has begun ..."

And when we had lit the candles He blessed the unleavened bread, the *Mazzot*, and broke it into many pieces. As He passed it round He said: *"Take, eat: this is my body which is given for you..."*

Likewise, having blessed the wine, He passed the cup round, and as He did so, said: *"Drink ye all of this, for this is my blood ..."*

Now, I know it was Mazzot that we ate, and yet it was not Mazzot.

I know it was wine that we drank, yet it was not wine.

It was as if His words had imbued them with His very substance; as if the I AM of which He had spoken so often had entered them and was now flowing through my flesh, my bones, my very blood and breath.

No-one spoke, and after some long while in that fulfilled silence He turned to Judah Ish Kiriot and said: "Go quickly and do what you must do."

Judah went very pale, but stood up at once, tried to stammer something, stopped himself, and with one last anguished look at Yeshua, stumbled past us and left the room.

No-one asked where Judah was going.

It was as if we were held under the spell of what had just taken place.

Then Yeshua said: "*Little children, yet a little while I am with you ... so now I say to you, that ye love one another; as I have loved you, that ye also love one another. By this shall all know that ye are my disciples, if ye love one another.*"

I saw the disciples look at each other, striving to pass beyond their personal dislikes and judgements of one another, with a longing to do what Yeshua commanded. I saw the coming and going of that different look in the eyes, nearer to Yeshua's unjudging, loving gaze ...

"Let us sing a hymn together before we part," He now said.

So we sang a psalm:

'I will lift up mine eyes unto the hills. From whence cometh my help?

My help cometh even from the Lord, who hath made heaven and earth.

He will not suffer thy foot to be moved; he that keepeth will not sleep.

Behold, he that keepeth Israel shall neither slumber nor sleep.

The Lord is thy keeper: the Lord is thy shade upon thy right hand.

The Lord shall preserve thee from all evil: he shall preserve thy soul.

The Lord shall preserve thy going out and thy coming in from this time forth and for evermore.'

Then he turned to us women, and said: "I wish you to stay here together, pray together and take your rest."

And to the disciples He said: "Come with me. Whatever comes to pass now, I want no anger, no violence from any one of you."

We all rose and with one last, long look at each one of us, He left us.

PART THREE - XV

'And he went forth with his disciples over the brook Cedron, where there was a garden, which he entered ...'

Two gardens were visited that night: one in the body, one in the spirit; one in agony, one in bliss ...

We only heard afterwards what happened in the first one, the garden on the Mount of Olives, called Gat Shemen. And that entirely thanks to the faithful servant, Eleazer, the only one to disobey his master's command, determined to remain near to him at all cost, until the end ...

Even now I can hardly bear to speak of it, to think of it ...

He had gone there to pray.

Keeping to the shadows, for the moon was up, Eleazer told us he followed Yeshua and the disciples into the garden, and heard his master tell them to wait for Him, except for Simon, Jacob and Jochanan. To them He said, "Come a little further with me *for my soul is exceeding sorrowful, even unto death. Tarry ye here, and watch with me ...*"

Then he moved a little distance from them but "not more than a stone's throw," Eleazer said, and began to pray.

And now Eleazer, through his tears, said, "He was so lonely. And do I betray Him now if I tell you what He said? Tell you that He was as full of fear as you or I would have been; that I heard Him pray: *'O father, if it be possible let this cup pass from my lips ...'*

"But then ... almost at once ... He was adding, *'nevertheless not as I will, but as <u>thou</u> wilt ...'*

"He was obeying, don't you see, obeying what He taught us in His prayer: *thy will be done* ...

"Twice He prayed thus, and in between he went back to the three and found that they had fallen asleep! At that very moment when He needed them, they had all fallen asleep.

"He spoke to them and they stirred and came half awake: *'Could ye not watch with me one hour? And this the Night of Watching. The spirit is willing, but the flesh is so weak ...'*

"He moved away again and prayed again, standing there, hands raised upwards, calling softly: *'Abba, father, If this cup may not pass away ... except I drink it, then thy will be done..'*

"And again he came and found Simon, Jacob and Jochanan asleep and I heard him say, in a voice of resignation, of acceptance, *'Sleep on and take your rest ...'*

"But while He was standing over them there was noise in the distance, noise growing nearer and louder all the time and the garden was suddenly lit up by great torches, blotting out the silver moon rays, and a great crowd began to appear, many of them armed with sticks and other weapons.

"The three woke up quickly enough then and leapt to their feet and encircled Yeshua, and the other disciples rushed forward and joined them. I could see they were all terrified.

"And now the crowd was right upon us and at the very front of it there was ... Judah! And he came straight up to Yeshua and kissed Him! Kissed Him, saying at the same time, 'This is the man you want ...'

Then Eleazer began to weep even more, so it was difficult to understand him, "But Yeshua was smiling at Judah, and I saw their eyes meet and something pass between them as if they both knew something that I did not ... and I think I heard Him call Judah *Friend* ..."

Suddenly I was back in our little house in Bethanehyeh on that day when Judah had come bursting in, seeking Maryam and I remembered what I had heard pass between them — remembered what I had so firmly pushed to the back of my mind that I had thought it truly forgotten ... *'I cannot.' 'Listen to him ... help him ... Do not fail him when the time comes ...'*

I felt cold, I trembled and my heart fluttered as if a thousand butterflies were flying there. I wondered if Maryam would say anything, try to console Eleazer by explaining that Judah had known and accepted his role, but she kept silent.

"There was a scuffle, Simon had got hold of a sword and was slashing at a soldier's face, cutting his ear badly. Yeshua rounded on the poor man and told him to drop the sword.

"Then they took Him away to the house and the court of Kaifa the High Priest, and I came here to you ... ."

"And the others all ran away," said Maryam.

Eleazer looked astonished. He could hardly look her in the eyes as he acknowledged this was so.

"But ... but," he added, "I think I saw Simon following at a distance ..."

"Yes," said Maryam. "I think you probably did ..."

And all that while we had been singing, singing the Song of Songs, in which the soul seeks — and finds and blends with the One; singing of another kind of garden, filled with the scents of flowers and fruit and the rich earth ... of life itself: *'The voice of my beloved! We will remember thy love more than wine ...; I am the rose of Sharon ... as the lily among thorns, so is my love among the daughters; as the apple tree among the trees of the wood, so is my beloved among the sons ...; my beloved spake and said unto me, Rise up, my love, my fair one and come away. For lo, the winter is past, the flowers appear ... the time of the singing of birds is come and the voice of the turtle is heard in the land ...; I am come into my garden; I sleep, but my heart waketh ... I am my beloved's and my beloved is mine ... he has gone down into his garden ... he feedeth among the lilies; set me as a seal upon thine heart, for love is strong as death ... many waters cannot quench love ... make haste, my beloved'.*

Two gardens, one of agony and darkness; the other of joy and light.

When Eleazer had left us, Maryam stood up and said calmly, "Let us do as my son asked. We have sung our hymn, now let us go to rest ..."

She held out her arms to us all, to me, to Martha, her sister, and the one from Magdala and enfolded us all in her blue robe.

As she let us go she said, "He will need us all."

Jenny Koralek

PART THREE - XVI

'Stabat mater ... '

Eleazer returned to us before noon the next day.

Poor man. His face was blotched red from running and white from shock and he poured with sweat.

"Fetch the mother! Fetch the mother!"

But she was already there and said, "He is to be crucified."

And it was not a question.

She knew.

She already knew.

We stared at her.

"I have seen it. I have seen it all.

"I have heard it all.

"I was with Him as He stood in front of the Council of the Elders.

"I heard their questions and His silence.

"I have seen Him taken, bound, from Kaifa's court to the hall of judgement.

"I was with Him when Pontius Pilate argued with our priests that He is a righteous man.

"I was there when he offered to release Him as they always release a prisoner at Passover.

"And I heard the crowd begin to grow mad and scream for Bar-Abbas to be set free — Bar-Abbas that well-known troublemaker and murderer ...

"I was with Him when Pontius Pilate asked Him, 'art thou King of the Jews?' and I heard Him answer, 'My kingdom is not of this world ... I came into this world that I should bear witness to the truth.'

"And heard Pontius Pilate laugh and say, 'Truth! What is truth?' and did not wait for an answer, but turned away and called for water in a bowl and a towel and washed his hands and said, 'You see? I wash my hands of this business. See <u>you</u> to it!'

"And I heard the crowd cry, 'Crucify him! Crucify him!', but I also saw many silent and weeping.

"I saw Pilate's soldiers press down a crown of thorns upon his head.

"I saw them whip Him, spit upon Him ...

"And yet I was not there, but alone in my room, opening my long-empty womb to Him, opening my heart up to Him, so much so that I was there with Him although in my room and it continues now.

"I have seen that good man from Cyrene shoulder my son's cross.

"I have seen poor Judah among that crowd — that crowd now jeering, now weeping, now groaning, now speechless. I have seen Judah and he has seen me, and turned away and vanished and I know he will be found hanged and none to mourn and few to understand ...

"Oh yes, I have seen the nails go in and heard His screams.

"You see, just as He said to us all, *'And lo, I AM with you always'*, so I am with Him because I am His mother and now I must go to Him ..."

PART THREE - XVII

'The cross, or whatever other heavy burden the hero carries, is himself, or rather the Self, his wholeness which is both God and animal ... the totality of his Being, which is rooted in his animal nature and reaches out beyond the merely human towards the divine. His wholeness implies a tremendous tension of opposites paradoxically at one with themselves, as in the Cross, their most perfect symbol.' (C G Jung)

'For it is right to mount upon the Cross of Christ, who is the Word stretched out ... of whom the spirit saith: For what else is Christ but the Word, the sound of God? So that the Word is the upright beam whereon I am crucified. And the sound is that which crosseth it, the nature of man. And the nail which holdeth the crosstree unto the upright in the midst thereof is the metanoia, the turning around of men.'
(Acts of Peter, Apocryphal New Testament)

It was a long way from Joseph's quiet house with its flower-filled courtyards to the hellish Golgotha, and I have always been ashamed of my relief that by the time we reached the ghastly place, Yeshua, His *kittel* still seamless but in tatters and bloody, had already been raised up, nailed to that cruelty, the cross and that He was all the time coming and going in and out of consciousness.

Maryam let out one sound, an echo of the animal noises women make while giving birth, but without faltering in her steps she moved to the foot of the cross, ignoring the rather weak attempt of the Roman centurion guarding it to stop her. For it was clear it was she who was in command and that nothing — no-one was going to stop her from being as close to her son as she could be.

I followed her with Maryam of Magdala, and we stationed ourselves one at each side with Martha and her sister close behind. The disciples and Eleazer were gathered at the other side of the cross.

I confess it took me some time to find the courage to look up, look at Him, but I heard Him murmur, "Beloved Mother ..."

Why is Martha fidgeting? I thought. Surely even she can see this is not a moment for activity, but I do her wrong: she was preparing in a little phial some myrrh which is close to the poppy in its ability to relieve pain and to distance the sufferer from it. She poured it onto a little sponge and bravely stepped forward and asked the centurion to put it on the end of his sword and offer it to Yeshua, which he did. But Yeshua feebly turned His head away. He would not take it. The centurion shrugged, but seemed disappointed. And Martha made a sound of angry distress.

We were far from alone up there on that hill. A huge crowd was still gathering as word must have got around that they were crucifying this 'King'. Hideous the way they stared; the relish at another's anguish, and yet I must be fair for there were others who soon turned away repulsed, disgusted and left; others who prayed; others who wept. But then someone called out: *'Go on, King! Why don't you call on Elijah to come and save you?' 'Yes!'* other voices joined in. *'Where is your father now?'*

It was then I became aware of Maryam's intense state: We seemed to be contained within a circle she was making, within which her atmosphere was charging itself with love, and that Yeshua, and all of us — even that kindly centurion — all of us were contained in an ever-increasing vibration coming from her, entirely focussed on her son.

Each time He came back into consciousness she held His eye with hers.

And then I saw that she was trying to draw off from her son the dark cloud of fear, the sharp shards of pain. She was sending towards Him her own light.

And then I saw that I was not alone in perceiving her intention: all the others were seeing it too.

Together we began to work with her towards this. The intention became visible in the form of light, a palpable substance, yet so fragile it could be broken by the touch of one fingertip — (I swear the centurion felt it too). Rays of light were emanating towards Him from the entire circle — the ones coming from His mother were the most visible, and never wavered in their strength. The others came and went as we all strove not to be overwhelmed by grief and terror.

And then He spoke: *Father, forgive them for they know not what they do ...* and fainted away again.

It was the longest of all mornings, the longest of all days.

Hour after hour we stood there, hour after hour we tried to watch faithfully, tried to sustain our efforts to be with Him. Hour after hour, he seemed on the point of leaving us — forever, as we thought then. Hour after hour He returned from wherever He had gone when another wave of agony swept over Him too hard to bear.

Once He lifted His head with very great difficulty and said, "Eleazer, from this day my mother is <u>your</u> mother," and after a long while turned it towards Maryam and said, "Mother, from this day Eleazer is your son ..."

Eleazer, weeping, said, "Rabbi ... Rabbi ..."

Dry-eyed, Maryam nodded slightly, completely focussed on her intention, not prepared to allow it to weaken, as if she was carrying precious water in her hands and none must be spilled.

And then came a terrible moment.

Suddenly Yeshua opened His eyes wide, turned upwards to the skies, so that we could see the whites of them, as if He was already more than halfway to death.

But no, He called out in the language of his childhood, and in a voice of such despair I pray daily for it to be erased from my memory ...

"Eli, eli, lama sabachtani?" which means, "My God, my God, why hast thou forsaken me?"

My heart began to beat rapidly. And my own despair began to set in. So, He, even He cannot after all transcend physical suffering, death.

But before the thought had time to lodge fixedly Maryam's voice rang out: *"For he hath not despised nor abhorred the affliction of the afflicted; neither hath he hid his face from him; but when he cried unto him, he heard ..."*

And I recognised the words they had both been speaking: they came from one of King David's psalms.

And I saw that Yeshua drew strength from them.

He seemed to surrender any remaining tension against all the pain of body and mind, and said simply in an almost child-like voice, *"I am thirsty."*

Immediately the centurion fetched water from a pitcher and offered some to Yeshua on Martha's sponge. And this time Yeshua sucked the sponge dry.

How much longer His agony continued after that I cannot tell, for on that day minutes became hours, hours became years.

But within those minutes which became hours; those hours which became days at last we heard Him sigh: *"Now it is fulfilled ..."*

And I swear I saw His life force vanish upwards through the body and leave through the topmost part of His head ...

Was it then that we were all held there outside time?

Was it then that I heard Him? Or did I dream this? Did we all dream the cross into a tree greening with leaves, sprouting with blossoms scenting the air?

Did we dream the voice? Did we dream Yeshua's voice and what we heard Him say?

"To all of you who love me I say: I have leaped and you have leaped with me. I am on the cross, yet I am not on the cross, but on this immortal tree, which is life. See! It stands in the middle of heaven and earth ... firm support of the universe, link between all things, a cosmic network, containing itself in all the medley of human nature. See! It is fixed by the invisible nails of the spirit ... I touch heaven with top of my head, I strengthen the earth with my feet and in the middle ground I embrace the whole atmosphere with my immeasurable hands ..."

Dream, vision, as swiftly as it had come, as swiftly it vanished and we were absorbed once more into the reality in front of us.

At the awful sound of the men's sobs as they struggled to remove the nails, Maryam fainted against me. The two of us began to fall slowly to the ground, and certainly would have fallen had it not been for the ready arms of the other women.

The centurion came rushing with his pitcher of water and helped us to seat her against a rock.

By the time the disciples had lifted Yeshua down from the cross, Maryam had come to herself and was trying to rise and go to Him. But she could not and sat back against the rock, holding her arms out to Him like a mother asking the midwife to lay her child in her eager arms.

So they brought Him to her, and laid Him across her knees. She cradled His head in her arms and began very carefully to lift the thorn crown off and to wipe the blood away with her cloak, washing the wounded forehead with her tears. For suddenly and at last Maryam was weeping.

"My babe, my child, my rabbi," she said again and again. "My babe, my child, my rabbi ..."

Then, looking up blindly, "Where to lay Him? Where to lay Him?"

"Do not fret yourself," said Martha in her sensible way. "That good man, Joseph, has thought of everything. See! He comes now with Pilate's permission to bury Him now, before Sabbath begins — <u>and</u> in the tomb he had prepared for himself ... Now, you come away home with us, dear mother, and leave the men to do what must be done."

Obediently Maryam allowed the men — Thomas, Simon, Eleazer and Jochanan to lift Yeshua up and prepare to carry Him away.

Obediently she allowed us to help her to her feet.

Then we stood back and waited, trying so hard not to weep aloud as she kissed Yeshua's brow, His hands, His feet. Although His eyes were already closed she made to close them with the soft palm of her hand.

"Thank you," she whispered. "Thank you." But only she knew who she was thanking: Joseph for giving his tomb? The men for carrying Him away to be bathed, anointed and robed in a shroud? Or was it Yeshua she was thanking? Or the Whole on High itself?

Jenny Koralek

PART THREE - XVIII

'Ave Maria, gratia plena ...'

I led her home on the donkey Joseph had thought to find for her.

I led her home, and suddenly I was back on the road into Egypt all those years ago, riding beside and sometimes, when the path was narrow, behind her. Then we held our babes close to us, beloved burdens. Now here we were — two old, childless women, carrying emptiness, loss, heavy, heavy loss under our hearts.

I led her home, while Martha and the other women hurried on ahead to light the Sabbath candles.

I have never forgotten the bearing of Maryam as she stepped down from that donkey at the door of that house in Bethanehyeh, which had been Yeshua's true home, heart and centre of His teaching.

Somewhere during our long, slow journey she had shed all vestige of her human nature and crystallised into that of the mother of all. She even seemed to have grown in stature, resembling more the form of <u>her</u> mother, who had always seemed slightly larger than life — as a goddess might in barely veiled disguise. She seemed filled again with an immense gravity. Even her beauty had in some way taken on a new depth: the eyes larger than ever, full of a new kind of love which embraced us all as we gathered round her. Her sadness which showed in them now encompassed all suffering and immense compassion. The sweet curve of her lips remained, but there was a firmness there made up of courage and resolve. Her back was straight again, her shoulders no longer hunched up in that posture we all make when we cringe against pain.

No, she stood there as Our Lady, Our Lady of Mercy, of Forgiveness, of Hope, of Grace, the Shekinah herself of our time, as Sarah had been of hers and those other mothers, Rebekah, Rachel, Leah, preparing their hearths for the Sabbath ...

"This Sabbath," she said to us, "must be purer and more wholehearted than ever before.

"Let it be truly worthy of the bride for whom it is prepared.

"Let the candles glow as if we had indeed lit them from the Divine Sparks.

"And let the door be opened wider than ever!"

And so it was.

But that night, that first night, it was my turn to take her into my bed; my turn to hold her, to warm her, to love her through her weeping, silent or loud.

She was up before sunrise and discovered all the disciples asleep on the floor, having found their way to Bethanehyeh, drawn there some time during the night, as if they knew it was the only place to be. She called us all together to watch the first rays spread up the sky.

And after the morning blessings had been said, the prayers recited, and bread broken and shared between us, she spoke to us.

"Sabbath is the holy space between the old and the new," she began. "Sabbath until now has been the holy space between the week which has passed and the new one to come. But this Sabbath day is also the holy space between the end of my son's life and a new beginning, where we must try to put into practice what He taught us — and He taught us enough and more for several lifetimes! This Sabbath we must together strike the first note of this new beginning. We all have engraved in our hearts, impressed upon our minds and in our very marrowbone the four things He taught us: ecstasy, service, humility, intention. And now is the time to activate intention as never before. So now, when we pray, truly wishing to direct our intention, we imagine that we are light and that everything around us is light, light from every direction and from every side. If we turn to the right we find shining light, and if we turn to the left we will find light and above us the crown of light which crowns the desires of the thoughts. This light is unfathomable, and from it comes grace and benevolence ..."

And so, due to her strength and presence we celebrated a vibrant Sabbath.

The portion from the Torah was from Moses — his great commandment, the commandment that is *"not hidden, neither far off, not in heaven that thou shouldest say, Who shall go up for us to heaven and bring it unto us, that we may hear it and do it?"* The commandment which is very near, in our mouths, and in our hearts that we may do it. *"See,"* he said to the children of Israel in their wilderness, *"I have set before thee this day <u>life and good</u>, and death and evil; in that I command thee this day to love the Lord thy God ... I call heaven and earth to record this day against you, that I have set before you life and death, blessing and cursing: <u>therefore choose life</u>."*

And the psalm for Passover was apt: *I love the Lord because he hath heard my voice and my supplication. The sorrow of death encompassed me: I found trouble and sorrow: I was brought low and he helped me.*

And the psalm of David to end with was one of praise: *O praise the Lord all ye people ... the truth of the Lord endureth forever. Praise ye the Lord ...*

The bride was welcomed with full and loving hearts.

That night both Maryam and I fell into deep and deeply needed sleep.

Jenny Koralek

PART THREE - XIX

'There He was, among them. He broke bread. He ate with them. Surely this transcends human experience. And yet it is to this rebirth that we are called, even before death. It can be given to us to experience this in our lifetime — by analogy.'
(Henri Tracol in *The Mystery of Rebirth*)

I awoke to find Maryam of Magdala, the sun's first rays fingering her hair, kneeling by the bed, a hand on Maryam's shoulder.

"Mother!" she was saying. "Mother! Wake up! Wake up!"

Maryam awoke immediately and said, "You've seen Him!"

"In the garden! I thought He was the gardener ..."

And then she wept — we all three wept with that great outpouring of joy which can only come after very great sorrow.

"I thought He was the gardener," the one from Magdala kept sobbing. Then, "I couldn't help it. I couldn't sleep, so I rose up and found Martha and her sister also awake, sitting in the dark. Suddenly Martha said, 'Let's go to Him! Let's go to our rabbi! We could at least stay near Him for a while and pray.' So we set off, slowly at first, but by the end we were running, running in our eagerness to be near Him again. Only as we drew near did Martha stop us and say, 'Best go quietly. We don't want any trouble with the guards.'

"But we need not have worried — they were all asleep. Of course, we had not expected to be able to enter the tomb. We knew of the large stone which had been rolled in front of the entrance. We <u>knew</u> they feared He would somehow be taken from there. But ..."

"The stone had been rolled away," said Maryam.

"So we peered in and were almost blinded by a great light. The others were frightened. 'We must run at once,' said Martha, 'and tell Simon and the others,' and they turned at once, but I did not go with them. I could not. I was frozen to the spot, still gazing into that great light, but it was too much to bear, so then I ran too, but through the garden, looking, looking for Him. I saw this man in the distance. The gardener, I thought ... Maybe <u>he</u> will have seen Him, so I called out as I ran towards him. 'Sir, sir! I seek my rabbi, my master. Did anyone come this way?'

"Then he turned.

"At once I knew it was Him, the beloved. But now translucent, transparent, a creature full of light and trailing light. Yeshua, His Being, His body no longer the envelope for this Being; His body now utterly and fully His Being, no longer an outer shell, but all one, barely a form; a subtle transformation, a new man, and yet always and forever my Yeshua, my beloved, my rabbi, my master. *'Rabboni!'* I heard myself cry out, and then, while knowing somehow that I must not touch Him, I put out my hand, longing to fling myself at His feet and kiss them when, 'No!' He said. 'Do not touch me! This new form, these new emanations, this immeasurable love which pervades me will be much too strong for you <u>now</u>. So go, Maryam of Magdala, go and tell my mother what deep within herself she already knows. Go and tell her and my cousin that I AM is risen. Go and tell Simon and all my dear ones that I will come to them, that they should all gather together in Bethanehyeh and I will come to them.'

"As He finished speaking I saw Him no more, but still there were shreds of light about the place where He had stood, although even without them I would have known this was no dream."

*****

He came to us that very evening. We had all gathered in great silence and great stillness at twilight — that mysterious moment where shade and shining meet — in the inner room of Bethanehyeh. I do not think any of us was fearful, but we sensed that we were taking part in a mystery which threatened to overwhelm us.

Suddenly He was there, there with us and looking just as Maryam of Magdala had described. There ... in the flesh, yet not as I, Elizabeth, in the flesh; not as we others were in the flesh, but reborn *in the flesh,* His form serving Him, showing us without a shadow of a doubt that it is possible — for some — to be reborn in the flesh.

His mother was first on her feet — gazing at Him, gazing. She stood there, her hands clasped to her lips.

"My child! My son! My rabbi!" she said. From the look that passed between them for some long while I saw that there was no need for them to embrace, but then Yeshua held out His arms to her.

"Imma! Imma! Imma, my beloved mother! Here am I!"

And she took His hands gently in hers and kissed the wounds.

Then He called each one of us by name, lastly Thomas, to whom He said, "Yes, my holy twin, come to me! You who have always carried my doubts for me, affirm for us both that I AM is here now in the flesh. Touch my hands! Touch my wounds!"

Weeping, Thomas obeyed, kissing the hands, the wounds on His side, His feet, His forehead, and at his touch they seemed to fade a little — not disappear, but fade.

"Peace be unto you," He said to us.

Then He breathed on us and said, "Receive this Holy Breath, receive **YHVH**."

And it is true — a true peace was there in me, and if in me, in all of us.

Holding out His arms, He said, "Here am I, fixed by invisible nails — the nails of the spirit. See! I touch heaven with the top of my head, strengthening the earth with my feet, and here in the middle ground I embrace the whole atmosphere with my immeasurable hands ... Did you hear me speak thus when I was on the cross?"

"Yes, my son," said Maryam.

"Yes, rabbi, yes," we all answered.

So what I had heard and seen at Golgotha was not a dream.

And then He taught us one last time, taught all of us in words so powerful that I burn from them still.

And was gone.

*****

Three more times He came to us: twice to the men and once to us women.

Two of the men met Him as they walked the road to Emmaeus and did not recognise Him; thought He was a stranger from some far off place, who seemed not to know of the terrible events in Jerusalem; joined Him for a meal at an inn, and then and only then, from the way He took the bread, broke it, blessed it and gave it to them did they realise who He was.

And one night when Simon, Thomas and some of the others were fishing, they saw Him on the shore, making a fire. Simon leapt from the boat and plunged his way towards Him through the water. He cooked for them some of the fresh fish, walked and talked alone with Simon, and as they turned to rejoin the others Simon realised he was alone.

He came also to us women.

To Martha He said, "You know your tasks, for you have been fulfilling them daily these many years. Martha, Martha, you are so much needed to keep the fire in the hearth at Bethanehyeh alight and brightly burning ..."

Turning to her sister, He said, "And you, Maryam, you now are ready to help her. As I was walking the road to you on the day your brother was re-born, I saw with my inner eye and sensed that you were moving to another possibility, so seize it now with both hands and a whole heart and help your sister, Martha, to hold high the pillars of the house, which will continue to see much life and action as the centre of my teaching. You virtuous women *whose price is far above rubies*, keep the roof raised high so that my disciples can go about their work ..."

Then He turned to Maryam of Magdala and said, "And you, my Maryam, you too already know your work. It will be hard, but the soil is well tilled. Just as Martha and her sister will blend the active way with the contemplative into the outer daily life, so you, and only you, can temper the men's urge *to do* with you women's urge *to be* in the inner daily life. They will not all at first welcome you. They will be rough with you and jealous, but I know that when at Pentecost my advocate, the Paraclete, the Holy Breath, comes down to dwell in you all for all time, there will be a melting, a dissolving of ordinary states, ordinary resistance, and you will all speak with a new voice from a new place."

To my Maryam He said, "And you, my dearest mother, I bow before you ..." And He did then and there. "You know better than I that you are <u>mother</u>, no longer just <u>my</u>mother, <u>my</u> atmosphere, the very atmosphere of boundless love, which sets no conditions, to all, immeasurably able to take all to your heart, to listen to all, to pray for all in the way you were taught so long ago at Bethanehyeh. No matter how weak the prayer they pray for themselves, or for others, they have only to call upon you: *Ave Maria, Mother of Mercy, Hope, Faith* — and you will take their cry into your heart and hold it up to the Whole on High and they will be given strength, for this is true comfort — strength and healing."

He fell silent and again a long look passed between mother and son, grave, vibrant, as if some very fine substance was being woven between them like a subtle cord never to be broken — as if the cord which had bound them until moments after His birth was once more being re-instated. It was like an embrace, a kiss without touching.

I was so moved I could not in the end bear to go on looking — it seemed anyway an intrusion — so I bowed my head and therefore received a great shock when He said, "And now, you, Elizabeth, dear cousin, I will never be far from you, because you have borne and will continue to bear a very hard but necessary part. I salute your utterly selfless devotion to my mother, Maryam, which is of the same degree and quality of faithfulness, conviction, humbleness and love as that which I received from your dear son, your Jochanan. There are some who seem always to have no memorial for their constancy and acts of kindness. But it will be known and remembered for all time that while we were both in our mothers' wombs you recognised Me, and your babe recognised Me and leapt for joy, and that it was you who first recognised my mother for who she was, and voiced the immortal and immense greeting: *Hail, Maryam, full of grace. Blessed are thou among women and blessed is the fruit of thy womb.*"

And then he came to me and <u>touched</u> me! Took my face in His hands and kissed me three times on the forehead ... Such light and heat filled me I felt myself to be on fire, the fire of His blessing, His acknowledgement, so that I knew I would be able to sustain and support my Maryam for the rest of my days.

So blinded was I by His light that I did not see Him go. It was the last time I saw Him until, until ... He came for her ...

Jenny Koralek

*****

All came to pass as He had said.

Martha, Maryam, with the faithful Eleazer, kept the house at Bethanehyeh open and welcoming for many years as the disciples came and went, bringing new groups of men and women seeking the wisdom of Yeshua.

A mantle of authority eventually settled upon Maryam of Magdala, and she became an honoured teacher and interpreter of Yeshua's teachings, generously sharing with us and the disciples the profound teachings and conversations she had had secretly and often with their master. But hers is a story in its own right and which was recorded not long before my Maryam's death — a copy brought to us fresh from the scribe's hand, a gospel which soars high above the literal accounts of Yeshua's teachings which, sad to say, were already being taught at a great remove from the true source, and also not sufficiently questioned.

And my Maryam?

Yes, she was mother. Mother to the Maryam from Magdala, to Simon, Jochanan, Jacob, Thomas and all the others. Mother accepted even by Martha; adored by the bereaved, the sick, the fearful and by those seekers, shy, tentative, who gained courage and clarity from her presence and the direct and simple way she was able to tell them what her son had taught. She drew vividly and accurately with her remarkable memory on His many parables — those exquisite stories He loved to tell which, because they were always about people we could all recognise, problems we had all faced, set in the landscape we lived in with its fruits and flowers, its vineyards and fig trees, its mustard seeds, its bread, its wine and wellsprings, we could all connect with at once and digest in our being as nourishing food and drink ...

But there came a time when she knew she needed to withdraw, to retire and to prepare herself for her own death.

She remained mostly in our room or in the little courtyard beneath the old fig trees. I was the only one allowed to come to her, to sit with her.

She took to dozing on and off throughout the day. At least, it seemed as if she were half asleep, but I felt that she was in fact very wide awake in some interior part of herself ... Pondering over all she had been through, all she had witnessed.

Often I sat nearby with my spindle or some other quiet task, watching over her, wondering where she was in her memories.

One afternoon she opened her eyes, and seeing me there, said, "Eva was with me. She said, 'Your task is done ... mother of the new Adam ... Take your rest.'

"I have dreams where the others appear coming and going, rather faint. It's as if they are all coming to say 'Good-bye' to me. Sarah kissed me and said, 'I too know what it is to sacrifice a son and then lose him ...'

"Rebekah said, 'Do you see him there? My Jacob, wrestling with the Whole on High?'

"Beautiful Rachel, too, came and spoke proudly of her Joseph, who brought his father Jacob and all his brethren out of a land of famine into a land of plenty ... 'You can say that your Yeshua has done for the spirit what my son did for the flesh ...'

"Sweet Ruth told me how each day of her life she blessed her mother-in-law for bringing her to love the Whole on High and reminded me that my dear Joseph descended from her line.

"But it has been the daughters of Job who touched me most. 'Our father would have greeted you with all honour,' they told me, 'recognising in you another who learned to stay there in front of the mystery of the Whole on High, stay there faithfully and persevere, however great the doubt ...'

"And they too kissed me ..."

"And Miriam?" I asked. "Does she come?"

"Oh, yes!" said Maryam. "She comes to remind me of her part in saving her brother Moses from certain death, and promises to dance for me when I cross the river ... Oh, Elizabeth, sometimes I am fearful when I think of my death ..."

I will never know where my words came from: "Never forget, my dear Maryam, *that we are loved.* I have only to turn my face upwards as a sunflower to the sun to feel the beneficence which is the Whole on High, vivifying all my being ..."

She nodded, and leaning over, took my hand and said, "Dear one, before I cross that river I must say to you that you could not mean more to me if you were my sister ..."

The tears began to trickle, but she had closed her eyes again and once more fallen into her dream, her sleep, her meditation.

PART THREE - XX

'I sing of a maiden who is matchless. King of all kings to her son she chose. He came all so still where His mother was, as dew in April which falleth on the grass. Mother and maiden never none but she. Well might such a lady God's mother be ...'

A few days later Maryam sitting thus in her chair, suddenly opened her eyes and cried out, "I saw Him! A young man just like Him, It <u>was</u> Him, and He was holding out a shroud ... my shroud ... I know now that He is coming for me Himself and I must be ready for Him!"

She withdrew then into the inmost room, and called Maryam of Magdala and me to her side, and asking us to sit nearby, she spoke to us gently, taking us each by the hand and saying, "I will be going soon. Do your work. Do His work to the very last day."

Then she lay down and fell into a sleep. It was not an ordinary sleep, but an attending on the final stages of her own death — the death without which the grain cannot break open and grow upwards. Of course, in her case the grain had long lain in deep and fallow earth, which had slowly, so very slowly transformed into a rich compost out of the suffering she had been called upon to endure, standing there watching the abuse her son was subjected to, the blood, the thorns, the nails, the jeers, the treachery of all kinds.

Like Him, she had to go down first — for three dark days and nights, down into her deep dark, a confrontation with herself, a confession to herself, a cleansing of herself. And then, too, like Him, her body would be re-born and then she too would ascend bodily and radiantly.

On the third day He came for her.

Came for *Our Lady; Notre Dame; Unsere Liebe Frau; Panaghia; Our Lady of Mercy, of Forgiveness, of Hope; Mater Dolorosa; Morning Star; Madonna della Stella; Madonna del Mare; Madonna della Misericordia; the Blessed Virgin Mary; Jungfrau Maria; Jomfru Maria; Container of the Uncontainable; Lady of the Angels; Most Honoured of the Cherubim; Mother ... Mother ... Mother ...*

Came that day again for <u>His</u> mother ...

Maryam! He called out to her, and she answered Him, saying: *Behold my child, my son, my rabbi, Here am I!*

How He loved her — perhaps never more than now! You could see it in the way He took her in His arms. But where once His little hands had clasped her neck, His face upturned, His cheek against hers, her arms now entwined around Him, her forehead leaned on His as tenderly He wrapped her, body and soul, in a mantle of light, kissing her and murmuring all the while: *O, my beloved Mother, arise, let us go hence.*

He came for her Himself, but He did not come alone. No, He came with the archangels Gabriel, and Raphael and Michael (but Samael, the archangel of death did not come).

He came with a host of angelic forms, cherubim and seraphim; with the flame-shaped light of the sun's rays; with the silver disc of the new moon; with the morning stars singing together. He came with Moses, Elijah, with Abraham and Isaac, and Jacob. He came with King David playing upon his sweet harp and singing, 'Mercy and truth are most surely met together in this Mother ...'; He came with Hannah, whose other name is Grace; he came with the Shekinah in the forms of Sarah, Rebekah, Leah and Rachel; He came with Eva, weeping tears of joy ... And the little room, the entire house of Bethanehyeh, the dwelling place of "I AM" was filled with a perfect fragrance which could only have come from that perfect garden we know exists from the Song of Songs.

And then He crowned His mother with a crown of roses, red and white, entwined with green, and little pearls gleamed from among the leaves and the whole of it was studded with stars, twelve of them. There came a rushing mighty wind and clouds which glowed gold and red. He set her upon the cloud, and joined her on it, and the host which had come down with Him surrounded the cloud, and the great wind swept them all upwards, and a light came down so bright we had to shield our eyes, and the mystery and the wonder of it all was so great that we had to fall to our knees, and only when all was quiet again did we dare to look about us. Once again the landscape which had become formless, nameless, was restored to the familiar earth and trees and stones and flowers. The birds were singing, the sky was blue again and no wind blew.

Maryam of Magdala and I rose slowly to our feet, unable to stop looking, looking upward, upward.

"She's gone," we said together dully, stupidly.

And turned, dazed, as if drunken, to join the other women and the many other followers of the disciples, gathered there with us, and Joseph of Arimathea and Rabbi Nicodemus.

But I could not help looking back one more time, looking up one more time and so I saw it, the sign, the evidence, the proof.

"Look! Look!" I cried out to the others so sharply that they all turned round immediately, and so saw what I could see — a great wonder, a great sign, a great ray descending from above. *And standing there a woman clothed with the sun, and the moon under her feet and upon her head a crown of twelve stars ...*

And the roses He had entwined in her hair were falling, falling downward and settling about us on the very earth where we were standing.

Jenny Koralek

ACKNOWLEDGEMENTS

Acknowledgements of sources consulted

The Holy Bible (King James Version and The New Jerusalem Bible)
The Apocryphal New Testament (M R James)
The Roman Catholic Missal
The Hebrew Prayer Book
The Haggadah

The Zohar
Judaism	I Epstein
Sabbath	A Heschel
Major Trends in Jewish Mysticism	G Scholem
Moses	M Buber
The Hebrew Tongue Restored	Fabre d'Olivet
The Thirteen-Petalled Rose	Adin Steinsaltz
The Gates of Light	Gikatilla
Kabbalah	Z'ev ben Shimon Halevi
The Nazarene	Scholem Asch
Spanning The Century	Tony Hare
The Nag Hammadi Library	ed. James Robinson
The Gospel of Thomas	
The Hymn of Jesus	
The Gospel of Mary Magdalene	
Sermons and Discourses	Meister Eckhart
The Cloud Upon The Sanctuary	Karl von Eckhartshausen
The Mystery of Rebirth	Henri Tracol
Lost Christianity	Jacob Needleman
All Hallow's Eve	Charles Williams
Kaleidoscope	Helen M Luke

Jenny Koralek

The Great Goddess	Anne Baring & Jules Cashford
The Jewish Sect of Qumran	
The Teachings of the Essenes	Edmond B Szekely
The Collected Works	C G Jung
The Christian Archetype	Edward Edinger
Icons & The Mystical Origins of Christianity	Richard Temple
The Poems	Gerard Manley Hopkins
The Poems	W B Yeats
To Live Within	Sri Anirvan
The Mathnawi	Rumi

And with grateful thanks to the late Tony Hare for sharing his lifelong study of Judaism.

www.ingramcontent.com/pod-product-compliance
Lightning Source LLC
Chambersburg PA
CBHW061322040426
42444CB00011B/2728